GoodFood
Sunday lunches

D1323072

10 9 8 7 6 5 4 3 2 1

Published in 2014 by BBC Books, an imprint of Ebury Publishing
A Random House Group company

The Random House Group Limited
Reg. No. 954009

Addresses for companies within the Random House Group can be found at www.randomhouse.co.uk

A CIP catalogue record for this book is available from the British Library

The Random House Group Limited supports the Forest Stewardship Council® (FSC®), the leading international forest-certification organisation. Our books carrying the FSC label are printed on FSC®-certified paper. FSC is the only forest-certification scheme supported by the leading environmental organisations, including Greenpeace. Our paper procurement policy can be found at www.randomhouse.co.uk/environment

To buy books by your favourite authors and register for offers visit www.randomhouse.co.uk

Printed and bound by Firmengruppe APPL, aprinta druck, Wemding, Germany
Colour origination by Dot Gradations Ltd, UK

Project Editor: Lizzy Gaisford
Designer: Kathryn Gammon
Production: Rebecca Jones
Picture Researcher: Gabby Harrington

ISBN: 9781849907859

MIX
Paper from
responsible sources
FSC® C004592

Picture credits

BBC *Good Food* magazine and BBC Books would like to thank the following people for providing photos. While every effort has been made to trace and acknowledge all photographers, we should like to apologise should there be any errors or omissions.

Peter Cassidy p111, p119, p117, p189; Will Heap p39, p81, p91, p101, p145; Lara Holmes p129; Dan Jones p139; Jonathan Kennedy p45, p155, p157, p211; Gareth Morgan p21, p23, p33, p43, p85, p173, p175; David Munns p13, p17, p25, p29, p35, p37, p41, p49, p57, p61, p65, p67, p71, p73, p75, p77, p105, p107, p109, p125, p131, p135, p141, p147, p161, p167, p169, p179, p191, p193, p199, p207, p209; Myles New p15, p19, p31, p59, p63, p87, p97, p201; Stuart Ovenden p47, p55, p69, p127, p151, p153, p171, p177, p181, p197; Lis Parsons p27, p89, p95, p137, p143; Craig Robertson p103, p113, p123, p159, p185; Maja Smend p115, p121, p165, p203; Sam Stowell p83, p133, p163; Philip Webb p11, p51, p53, p79, p93, p99, p149, p183, p187, p195, p205

All the recipes in this book were created by the editorial team at *Good Food* and by regular contributors to BBC Magazines.

weekend

GoodFood
Sunday lunches

Editor **Cassie Best**

Contents

Introduction

For many of us, Sunday lunch is the most important meal of the week as we get to catch up with friends and family over a lovingly prepared meal. Whether you're cooking for 2 or 10, it's a nice opportunity to push the boat out and make something special.

As well as classic, guaranteed crowd pleasers, delicious dishes for veggies and recipes to impress your guests, we've included lots of lovely sides in each chapter, so you can mix and match for the best flavour combinations.

If you want to make a Sunday lunch with a difference we've included a chapter jam-packed with ideas for spicing up your roast, be it with warming Indian spices, or in a Chinese braised beef pie. Plus there are some inspiring ideas for sides with a twist.

While feeding a crowd is enjoyable, large joints of meat can be very expensive, so we've also included a chapter for cooking on a budget. And although we've managed to stretch the meat a little further with clever dishes like our sausage and stuffing toad-in-the-hole, these dishes are often the tastiest and will guarantee clean plates all round!

Sunday lunch wouldn't be complete without a comforting bowl of homemade pudding. In our desserts chapter you'll find something sweet for any Sunday lunch occasion – just add lashings of hot custard!

As always, all of the recipes in this book have been triple-tested in the *Good Food* kitchen, so you can rest safe in the knowledge that they will work first time, and every time, in your kitchen too.

Cassie

Cassie Best
Good Food magazine

Notes and conversion tables

NOTES ON THE RECIPES

• Eggs are large in the UK and Australia and extra large in America unless stated otherwise.

• Wash fresh produce before preparation.

• Recipes contain nutritional analyses for 'sugar', which means the total sugar content including all natural sugars in the ingredients, unless otherwise stated.

OVEN TEMPERATURES

Gas	°C	°C Fan	°F	Oven temp.
¼	110	90	225	Very cool
½	120	100	250	Very cool
1	140	120	275	Cool or slow
2	150	130	300	Cool or slow
3	160	140	325	Warm
4	180	160	350	Moderate
5	190	170	375	Moderately hot
6	200	180	400	Fairly hot
7	220	200	425	Hot
8	230	210	450	Very hot
9	240	220	475	Very hot

APPROXIMATE WEIGHT CONVERSIONS

• All the recipes in this book list both imperial and metric measurements. Conversions are approximate and have been rounded up or down. Follow one set of measurements only; do not mix the two.

• Cup measurements, which are used by cooks in Australia and America, have not been listed here as they vary from ingredient to ingredient. Kitchen scales should be used to measure dry/solid ingredients.

Good Food is concerned about sustainable sourcing and animal welfare. Where possible humanely reared meats, sustainably caught fish (see fishonline. org for further information from the Marine Conservation Society) and free-range chickens and eggs are used when recipes are originally tested.

SPOON MEASURES

Spoon measurements are level unless otherwise specified.

- 1 teaspoon (tsp) = 5ml
- 1 tablespoon (tbsp) = 15ml
- 1 Australian tablespoon = 20ml (cooks in Australia should measure 3 teaspoons where 1 tablespoon is specified in a recipe)

APPROXIMATE LIQUID CONVERSIONS

metric	imperial	AUS	US
50ml	2fl oz	¼ cup	¼ cup
125ml	4fl oz	½ cup	½ cup
175ml	6fl oz	¾ cup	¾ cup
225ml	8fl oz	1 cup	1 cup
300ml	10fl oz/½ pint	½ pint	1¼ cups
450ml	16fl oz	2 cups	2 cups/1 pint
600ml	20fl oz/1 pint	1 pint	2½ cups
1 litre	35fl oz/1¾ pints	1¾ pints	1 quart

Mustard-glazed roast chicken with Waldorf stuffing

Transform a classic roast chicken with a mustard glaze and a fruity stuffing of apple, celery and walnuts, inspired by the famous Waldorf salad.

TAKES 2 HOURS • SERVES 4–6

1 large chicken (about 2kg/4lb 8oz)
25g/1oz butter
1 tbsp wholegrain mustard
roast potatoes and veg, to serve
    (optional)

FOR THE STUFFING

3 celery sticks, finely chopped
2 red apples, cored and finely chopped
100g/4oz walnuts, chopped
100g/4oz fresh breadcrumbs, handful
    reserved for the topping
400g/14oz sausagemeat or about
    6 sausages
1 medium egg
handful parsley leaves, chopped
2 tbsp wholegrain mustard
25g/1oz butter, plus extra for greasing

1 Heat oven to 190C/170C fan/gas 5. To make the stuffing, mix together all the ingredients, except the butter, in a large bowl with some seasoning. Scrunch with your hands until well combined.

2 Season the chicken all over and put in a roasting tin. Smear with the butter and place on the middle shelf of the oven for 50 minutes.

3 Meanwhile, grease a 20 x 30cm roasting tin. Press in the stuffing, then sprinkle with the reserved breadcrumbs and dot with the butter.

4 Brush the chicken with the mustard, transfer it to a lower shelf and roast for 40 minutes more until cooked through and the juices run clear. Put the stuffing on the top shelf at the same time and cook for 40–50 minutes until crisp.

5 Leave the chicken to rest for 10 minutes, then serve with the stuffing, along with roast potatoes and veg, if you like.

PER SERVING (6) 734 kcals, protein 45g, carbs 21g, fat 52g sat fat 16g, fibre 3g, sugar 6g, salt 2.5g

Rolled pork belly with herby apricot stuffing

Who doesn't love crispy shards of crackling with their roast pork?

TAKES 3½ HOURS, PLUS CHILLING

● **SERVES 6–8**

4 tbsp olive oil

1 onion, chopped

2.25kg/5lb piece pork belly, boned and skin on

50g/2oz fresh breadcrumbs

small bunch parsley, chopped

small handful thyme, leaves picked

10 sage leaves, chopped

140g/5oz dried apricots, chopped

1 tbsp flaky sea salt

2 tbsp clear honey

1 Heat 1 tablespoon of the oil in a small frying pan. Add the onion and cook for 10 minutes until golden. Trim off 100g/4oz of the pork, from the meaty side. Whizz the trimmings in a food processor. Season and mix in a bowl with the breadcrumbs, herbs, apricots, onion and half of the oil.
2 Turn the pork belly skin-side up. Score the skin at 1cm/½in intervals and rub the sea salt all over. Turn the pork belly over, season, then brush with the honey. Lay the stuffing down the centre, then bring the two ends together and roll tightly. Flip the pork over so the ends meet underneath. Secure with kitchen string. Put on a wire rack in a roasting tin. Leave in the fridge, uncovered, for 3–24 hours.
3 Heat oven to 200C/180C fan/gas 6. Rub the pork with the remaining oil and roast for 30 minutes. Turn the oven down to 180C/160C fan/gas 4 and cook for 2½ hours. To crisp the skin, place it under a hot grill for 5–10 minutes, turning every 2 minutes. Remove from the heat, cover tightly with foil and rest before serving.

PER SERVING (8) 715 kcals, protein 52g, carbs 17g, fat 49g, sat fat 16g, fibre 2g, sugar 12g, salt 2.5g

Roast lamb with spring-herb crumbs

This roast leg of lamb makes the perfect centrepiece for an Easter gathering.

TAKES 2 HOURS 20 MINUTES

● **SERVES 8**

FOR THE LAMB

5 carrots, cut into chunks

2 onions, cut into chunks

4 bay leaves

small bunch rosemary

2 tbsp olive oil

large leg of lamb (about 3kg/6lb 8oz)

3 garlic cloves, thickly sliced, plus a
　　whole bulb, halved

FOR THE GRAVY

5 tbsp plain flour

200ml/7fl oz white wine, plus a splash

600ml/1 pint lamb stock

FOR THE CRUMBS

100g/4oz good-quality white bread

2 garlic cloves

zest 1 lemon

1 tsp thyme leaves, chopped

small bunch parsley, chopped

3–4 anchovy fillets, chopped (optional)

1 Heat oven to 160C/140C fan/gas 3. Scatter the vegetables, bay leaves and a few rosemary sprigs into a large roasting tin and drizzle with the olive oil. Make slits all over the lamb and poke a slice of garlic and a sprig of rosemary into each one. Sit the lamb on top of the veg, add a splash of the gravy wine. Cook for 2–2½ hours, to your liking. Transfer the lamb from the oven to a board and cover with foil. Rest for 45 minutes–1 hour.

2 Pour off most of the fat from the tin, leaving the veg and meat juices. Place the tin on the heat to caramelise the veg, then stir in the flour and cook to a paste. Stir in the wine and cook for a minute. Stir in the stock and simmer. Sieve the gravy into a small pan and keep warm.

3 Turn oven to 220C/200C fan/gas 7. For the crumbs, blitz everything in a food processor and scatter in a tin. Bake for 10–15 minutes.

4 Serve the lamb sprinkled with crumbs, with a jug of gravy and some veg.

PER SERVING 532 kcals, protein 45g, carbs 18g, fat 30g, sat fat 12g, fibre 2g, sugar 5g, salt 0.6g

Spiced roast beef with red-wine gravy

A fillet of beef makes the perfect roast for a special occasion lunch.

TAKES 1 HOUR 35 MINUTES

● **SERVES 6–8**

2 tbsp mixed peppercorns

2 tbsp mustard seeds, yellow or black, or 1 tbsp of each

2 tsp fennel seeds

1.5kg/3lb fillet of beef

1 tbsp wholegrain or English mustard

2 tbsp Dijon mustard

2 tbsp olive oil

3 red onions, skins left on, thickly sliced into rounds

a few thyme leaves, to scatter (optional)

FOR THE GRAVY

2 tbsp olive oil

1½–2 tbsp cornflour

2 beef stock cubes

3–4 tbsp redcurrant jelly

400ml/14fl oz red wine

1 Up to 2 days before, crush together the peppercorns and seeds using a pestle and mortar. Brush the beef fillet all over with the mustard, then roll in the peppercorn mix to coat. Cover and chill.

2 Take out of the fridge and leave for 2 hours to come to room temperature.

3 Heat oven to 200C/180C fan/gas 6. Heat the oil in a large pan and brown the beef all over, seasoning with salt. In a roasting tin, use the onions as a bed to sit the beef on. Roast for 20 minutes for rare, 25 minutes for medium and 35 minutes for well-done. Put the beef on a platter, rest, covered with foil, for 30 minutes.

4 Set the tin with the onions and roasting juices over the hob and stir in the oil and cornflour, and crumble in the stock cubes. Mix in the jelly, then gradually stir in the wine and 400ml/14fl oz boiling water. Simmer for 15 minutes until reduced a little. Season, then sieve into a clean pan to keep warm, discarding the onions. Slice the beef, scatter over the thyme, if you like. Serve with the gravy.

PER SERVING (6) 544 kcals, protein 54g, carbs 16g, fat 26g, sat fat 9g, fibre 1g, sugar 8g, salt 1.4g

Lemony roast-chicken pie

This pie uses a roast chicken and the juices from the pan for a wonderful flavour.

TAKES 4¼ HOURS ● SERVES 6

2 lemons, halved
1 large chicken (about 1.8kg/4lb)
25g/1oz softened butter
2 celery sticks, diced
1 onion, diced
1 large fennel bulb, diced
50g/2oz plain flour, plus extra for
    dusting
500ml/18fl oz chicken stock
200ml pot single cream
small bunch parsley, chopped
500g/1lb 2oz pack all-butter shortcrust
    pastry
1 egg, beaten with a fork

1 Heat oven to 200C/180C fan/gas 6. Push the lemon halves inside the chicken then sit it in a roasting tin, smear butter over the breasts and season. Roast, breast-side up, for 30 minutes, then turn over and roast for 1½ hours until cooked.
2 With 30 minutes to go, pour the juices from the tin into a jug. Once it has separated, spoon 50ml/2fl oz fat from the top into a pan. Add the celery, onion and fennel, and soften for 20 minutes.
3 On the heat, stir the flour into the veg until absorbed. Stir in the chicken juices and stock, and simmer. Stir in the cream and parsley, take off the heat and season.
4 Shred the chicken, discarding the skin. Juice the roasted lemons and stir all the juices and roasted pulp into the sauce with the chicken. Tip into a pie dish.
5 Roll out the pastry on a floured surface until big enough to cover the pie. Brush the dish rim with egg and lift on the pastry. Trim the edges, then press and crimp to seal. Brush all over with egg and bake for 30–40 minutes until golden.

PER SERVING 754 kcals, protein 34g, carbs 46g, fat 48g, sat fat 17g, fibre 4g, sugar 4g, salt 1.4g

Italian-style turkey crown with roast garlic

Turkey shouldn't just be saved for Christmas – this lean, tasty meat is a great choice to feed a crowd for any Sunday lunch of the year.

TAKES 2 HOURS 35 MINUTES

● **SERVES 6–8**

2–2.5kg/4lb 8oz–5lb 8oz turkey crown
drizzle olive oil
about 10 thin slices streaky bacon or pancetta
small rosemary sprigs
1 large onion, cut into 8 wedges
3 whole bulbs garlic, halved horizontally
1 lemon, cut into 6 wedges

1 Heat oven to 190C/170C fan/gas 5. Weigh the turkey to calculate the cooking time: allow 20 minutes per kg, plus 70 minutes. Rub the turkey all over with olive oil and season. Lay the bacon or pancetta over the top. Insert rosemary between the slices. Tie the crown in 3–4 places with butcher's string. Put the onion wedges in a large roasting tin and sit the crown on top. Cover with a loose tent of foil, then roast according to your calculated time.

2 With 30 minutes to go, remove the turkey and increase oven to 200C/180C fan/gas 6. Remove the foil, place the garlic and lemon around the turkey. Return to the oven and continue to roast for the final 30 minutes. To test if cooked, pierce the fattest part of the crown with a skewer – the juices should run clear. If they are pink, continue to roast, checking at 10-minute intervals. Rest for 30 minutes before carving.

PER SERVING (8) 452 kcals, protein 76g, carbs 4.4g, fat 15g, sat fat 5g, fibre 1.2g, sugar 2g, salt 0.9g

Cottage pie

This family favourite is made even better with a cheesy-mash topping. This recipe makes two pies: one for now and one for the freezer.

TAKES 2 HOURS 25 MINUTES

● **SERVES 10**

3 tbsp olive oil

1.25kg/2lb 12oz beef mince

2 onions, finely chopped

3 carrots, chopped

3 celery sticks, chopped

2 garlic cloves, finely chopped

3 tbsp plain flour

1 tbsp tomato purée

large glass red wine

850ml/1½ pints beef stock

few thyme sprigs

2 bay leaves

4 tbsp Worcestershire sauce

FOR THE MASH

1.8kg/4lb potatoes, chopped

225ml/8fl oz milk

25g/1oz butter

200g/7oz strong Cheddar, grated

freshly grated nutmeg

1 Heat 1 tablespoon of the oil in a large pan and fry the mince in batches until browned. Set aside. Put the rest of the oil into the pan, add the vegetables and cook on a gentle heat until soft, about 20 minutes. Add the garlic, flour and tomato purée, increase the heat and cook for a few minutes, then return the beef to the pan. Pour over the wine and boil to reduce before adding the stock, herbs and Worcestershire sauce. Simmer, uncovered, for 45 minutes. Season. Discard the bay leaves and thyme stalks.

2 Boil the potatoes in a large pan, and simmer until tender. Drain, then steam-dry. Mash with the milk, butter and ¾ of the cheese. Season with the nutmeg.

3 Heat oven to 220C/200C fan/gas 7. Spoon the meat into two ovenproof dishes then cover with mash. Sprinkle with the remaining cheese. Cook for 25–30 minutes, or until golden. To freeze, wrap (unbaked) in foil. Store for 2 months.

PER SERVING 600 kcals, protein 37g, carbs 40g, fat 34g, sat fat 16g, fibre 4g, sugar 7g, salt 1.15g

Apricot & ginger ham

This ham is delicious served hot or cold. It can be baked a day or two before it is needed and served cold with homemade salads, or hot as part of a Sunday roast.

TAKES 3 HOURS 40 MINUTES
- **SERVES 15–20**

4–5kg/11lb raw smoked ham on the bone (ask your butcher if your ham needs to be soaked before cooking – some are pre-soaked to save you time)
2-litre bottle ginger beer
2 bay leaves
6 whole allspice berries
6 black peppercorns
30–40 whole cloves
1 tsp ground ginger
340g jar apricot jam

1 If needed, soak the ham. In a large pan, cover with water, and leave in the fridge for 24 hours. Change the water twice.
2 Pour away the soaking water and rinse the pan. Return the ham to the pan and add the ginger beer, bay leaves, allspice, peppercorns and 6 of the cloves. Top up with water to cover the ham. If the bone sticks out of the liquid, rotate the ham halfway through. Simmer over a medium heat, then cover with a lid. Leave to cook for 2½ hours, topping up with water.
3 Heat oven to 200C/180C fan/gas 6. Discard the liquid and pat the ham dry with kitchen paper. Use a sharp knife to pare the rind away from the ham, leaving a layer of fat attached to the meat. Score the fat in a diamond pattern and stud with the remaining cloves. Put the ham in a roasting tin. Mix together the ginger and jam, and brush the mixture all over. Roast for 1 hour until golden. Serve hot or cold.

PER SERVING (20) 343 kcals, protein 33g, carbs 13g, fat 18g, sat fat 6g, fibre none, sugar 13g, salt 4.3g

Make-ahead gravy

With this recipe up your sleeve, you'll always have enough gravy to go around for a big family meal, such as Christmas lunch.

TAKES 1 HOUR 20 MINUTES

● **SERVES 8**

1kg/2lb 4oz chicken wings, halved with kitchen scissors

the turkey neck, if you have it, cut into pieces (optional)

3 large carrots, chopped into chunks

2 onions, unpeeled and chopped

3 celery sticks, chopped

small handful thyme sprigs

2 tsp golden caster sugar

2 tbsp sunflower oil

1 tbsp tomato purée

4 tbsp plain flour

4 tbsp balsamic vinegar

1 vegetable stock cube

1 Heat oven to 220C/200C fan/gas 7. Tip the chicken wings into a roomy roasting tin with the turkey neck (if using), carrots, onions, celery and thyme. Scatter over the sugar, toss in the oil and roast for 50 minutes until brown and lightly charred.

2 Boil the kettle. Put the roasting tin over a low heat, stir in the tomato purée and flour, and cook until sticky. Splash in the vinegar, then pour over 1.5 litres/2½ pints water to just cover all the ingredients. Bring to a simmer. Crumble in the stock cube and use a potato masher to mash all the ingredients together to release the flavour.

3 Simmer everything for 20 minutes until you have a tasty thickened gravy, then strain it through a sieve, pushing down hard on all the mushy veg. Cool and chill for up to 3 days, or freeze for up to 3 months.

4 Heat the gravy to serve, adding the juices from your roasted bird, if you like.

PER SERVING 166 kcals, protein 11g, carbs 15g, fat 6g, sat fat 1g, fibre 2g, sugar 7g, salt 0.5g

Apricot & pecan stuffing

Use this versatile stuffing moulded into balls, baked flat in a tray, stuffed into a chicken or turkey, or rolled up in a joint of pork.

TAKES 45 MINUTES ● MAKES 4 BATCHES OF 24 PORTIONS

50g/2oz butter
2 onions, halved and sliced
4 celery sticks, chopped
200g/7oz semi-dried apricots, halved
3 garlic cloves, chopped
140g/5oz pecan nuts, roughly broken
1 tsp ground nutmeg
200g/7oz fresh breadcrumbs
500g/1lb 2oz pork mince
1 large egg
3 tbsp chopped soft thyme leaves
good handful chopped parsley leaves

1 Melt the butter in a large pan, add the onions and celery, and cook briefly until they start to soften. Stir in the apricots and garlic, and cook for a few minutes more. Finally, add the pecans and nutmeg, and cook, stirring, until the nuts are lightly toasted. Cool.

2 Stir in the breadcrumbs, pork mince, egg and herbs with 1 teaspoon salt and lots of black pepper, then divide the mixture into four, pack into bags and freeze. It will keep for 3 months.

3 To use, defrost in the fridge overnight. If making stuffing balls, roll the stuffing into walnut-size balls and bake at 200C/180C fan/gas 6 for 25 minutes. Alternatively, use to stuff a chicken, turkey or boned pork shoulder or leg.

PER PORTION 143 kcals, protein 6g, carbs 11g, fat 8g, sat fat 2g, fibre 2g, sugar 5g, salt 0.5g

Salt & pepper roasties

Golden, crispy roast potatoes are a must for any Sunday lunch. Make sure you use a floury potato for nice crispy edges: King Edwards are best.

TAKES 1 HOUR 35 MINUTES

● **SERVES 8**

2kg/4lb 8oz King Edward or Maris Piper potatoes
6 tbsp goose fat
2 tbsp plain flour
flaky sea salt
½ tbsp black peppercorns, crushed
6 tbsp vegetable oil

1 Heat oven to 180C/160C fan/gas 4. Cut the potatoes into halves, quarters or eighths if really large – you want to end up with even-sized 5cm/2in pieces. Put the potatoes in a large pan of salted water. Bring to the boil, then simmer for 8–10 minutes, until the outsides start to soften. To check, try scraping a potato with a fork – it should be easy to make a mark but you shouldn't be able to slide it into the flesh. Drain really well, then shake in the pan to rough the potatoes up a bit. Add the goose fat, flour, salt and crushed peppercorns, and toss until coated.

2 Place the oil in a roasting tin large enough to hold all the potatoes in one layer and heat in the oven for 5 minutes. Quickly tip the potatoes in and return to the oven. Cook for 30 minutes, turning once. Increase oven to 200C/180C fan/gas 6. Cook for 30–40 minutes more or until crisp all over. Sprinkle with extra salt to serve.

PER SERVING 360 kcals, protein 6g, carbs 43g, fat 18g, sat fat 4g, fibre 3g, sugar 1g, salt 0.3g

Herby-mustard Yorkies

The secret to perfect, puffed-up Yorkshire puddings is not to open the oven before the cooking time is up – if you do, the heat will escape, and they will sink.

TAKES 30 MINUTES • MAKES 12

200g/7oz plain flour
2 large tbsp English mustard powder
5 large eggs
400ml/14fl oz milk
large bunch rosemary and thyme,
    leaves picked
4 tbsp sunflower oil

1 Heat oven to 220C/200C fan/gas 7. In a bowl, beat the flour and mustard powder with the eggs until you have a smooth, thick batter. Gradually beat in the milk until the batter is the same consistency as single cream, then stir in the herbs and season.

2 Pour a drizzle of oil into each hole of a sturdy 12-hole muffin tin. Put the tin in the oven and heat for 5 minutes. Working quickly, remove the tin and pour enough batter into each hole so that it comes two-thirds of the way up the sides. Carefully place the tin back in the oven and cook the puddings for about 20 minutes until they are puffed up and brown.

PER YORKIE 157 kcals, protein 7g, carbs 16g, fat 8g, sat fat 2g, fibre 1g, sugar 2g, salt 0.13g

Mulled red cabbage with clementines

This Christmassy favourite is enhanced with mulling spices and clementine zest. Great with chicken, turkey, ham or game birds.

TAKES 1¼ HOURS • SERVES 6

4 clementines (or satsumas or mandarins), 1 left whole, zest and juice from 3
15 whole cloves
700g/1lb 9oz chunk red cabbage, finely shredded
2 red onions, chopped
200ml/7fl oz red wine vinegar
140g/5oz brown sugar
1 tsp ground mixed spice

1 Stud the whole clementine with the cloves and set aside.

2 Mix the remaining ingredients in a big pan with a lid or a flameproof casserole. Cover and cook for 30 minutes, then snuggle in the studded clementine, cover again and cook for 30 minutes more until the cabbage is tender. Season and eat hot or at room temperature.

PER SERVING 138 kcals, protein 2g, carbs 31g, fat 1g, sat fat none, fibre 4g, sugar 30g, salt 0.1g

Honey-glazed roast carrots

Roasting your carrots instead of boiling them will bring out their sweet, earthy flavour and give them lovely sticky edges.

TAKES 1 HOUR • SERVES 8

1kg/2lb 4oz Chantenay or other small
   carrots, peeled
3 tbsp sunflower oil
2 tbsp white wine vinegar
2 tbsp clear honey

1 Heat oven to 190C/170C fan/gas 5. Tip the carrots into a roasting tin and toss with the oil and some salt and pepper. Roast for 30 minutes.
2 Drizzle the vinegar and honey over the carrots, toss well and return to the oven for a further 20 minutes.

PER SERVING 85 kcals, protein 1g, carbs 10g, fat 5g, sat fat 1g, fibre 3g, sugar 10g, salt 0.13g

Creamy cauliflower & broccoli bake

Cauliflower and broccoli florets served in a creamy sauce, topped with crisp crumbs. This is sure to become a firm-favourite side dish to serve alongside a roast dinner.

TAKES 45 MINUTES ● SERVES 8

1 large cauliflower, broken into florets
1 vegetable stock cube
1 large broccoli, broken into florets
200g tub crème fraîche
1 tbsp wholegrain mustard
splash white wine (optional)
generous grating nutmeg
2 slices stale bread, whizzed into
  crumbs

1 Put the cauliflower in a large pan and cover with cold water, add the stock cube, then bring to the boil. Add the broccoli and cook for 1 minute, then drain (reserving some of the stock) and allow to steam-dry for 1–2 minutes. (The veg shouldn't be tender.)

2 Heat oven to 200C/180C fan/gas 6. Mix together the crème fraîche, mustard, wine (if using), nutmeg, enough reserved stock to make a white sauce consistency and some seasoning. Add the veg and mix well. Tip into an ovenproof dish, scatter with the breadcrumbs and bake for 30 minutes until golden and crisp on the top.

PER SERVING 173 kcals, protein 8g, carbs 8g, fat 12g, sat fat 7g, fibre 5g, sugar 4g, salt 0.6g

Chipolatas wrapped in sage & pancetta

Serve these moreish pancetta-wrapped chipolatas alongside a roast chicken to stretch it a little further.

TAKES 30 MINUTES • MAKES 24

24 slices pancetta
24 whole sage leaves
24 chipolata sausages
oil, for greasing

1 Heat oven to 220C/200C fan/gas 7. Put 1 slice of the pancetta on a chopping board and stretch out using the back of a knife. Put 1 of the sage leaves and 1 of the sausages on top, and roll the sausage up on the diagonal, covering all of it.

2 Put the wrapped sausage on a lightly greased baking sheet and repeat with the remaining sausages. These can be prepared and chilled 2 days ahead. Cook for 20–25 minutes until crisp and cooked through.

PER WRAPPED CHIPOLATA 103 kcals, protein 6g, carbs 2g, fat 8g, sat fat 3g, fibre none, sugar 1g, salt 0.6g

Creamy potato gratin with caramelised onions

This indulgent potato gratin is flavoured by sweet, caramelised onions. Make sure you cook them until deep golden brown for best results.

TAKES 2¾ HOURS • SERVES 8

2 tbsp olive oil
2 onions, thinly sliced
2 thyme sprigs, leaves picked, plus
    extra sprig to garnish
150ml/¼ pint double cream
175ml/6fl oz milk, plus a splash
1.25kg/2lb 12oz large potatoes, peeled
    and thinly sliced
butter, for greasing
100g/4oz crème fraîche
85g/3oz Parmesan, grated

1 Heat oven to 200C/180C fan/gas 6. Heat the oil in a large frying pan. Add the onions and thyme, cover, and cook over a gentle heat for 10–15 minutes until softened and caramelised. Pour the cream and milk into a large bowl and season well. Add the potatoes and mix to combine.

2 Butter a 23 x 28cm ovenproof dish, then layer in half the potatoes. Spread the onion mixture on top, then layer on the remaining potatoes. Press down with your hands. Pour over the milk mixture, which should come just level with the potatoes. If not, add a splash more milk until it does. Cover with foil, then bake for 1½ hours until tender.

3 Increase oven to 220C/200C fan/gas 7. Uncover, spread the crème fraîche on top, then sprinkle over the Parmesan. Cook for 30 minutes until the cheese is melted, the top is crisp and golden brown, and the gratin is piping hot. Serve garnished with extra thyme.

PER SERVING 357 kcals, protein 9g, carbs 31g, fat 23g, sat fat 12g, fibre 3g, sugar 4g, salt 0.29g

Steamed venison & port pudding

This rich venison pudding will steam away happily for a few hours on a Sunday afternoon, leaving you time to read the papers and relax.

TAKES 4 HOURS 40 MINUTES

● **SERVES 4**

FOR THE PASTRY

375g/13 oz self-raising flour

140g/5oz beef suet

oil or lard, for greasing

FOR THE FILLING

2 tbsp dripping or lard

600g/1lb 6oz cubed stewing venison (trimmed shoulder is best)

140g/5oz cubed pork belly, skin on

1 onion, finely sliced

1 tbsp plain flour

1 tsp thyme leaves, chopped

1 bay leaf

2 tbsp mushroom ketchup

100ml/3½fl oz port

50ml/2fl oz red wine

125ml/4fl oz good beef stock

1 To make the pastry, mix the flour, 1 teaspoon salt and the suet. Add 250ml (9fl oz) cold water and mix to a dough.

2 Melt the dripping for the filling in a large pan. Brown the venison and pork. Remove the meat to a bowl. Add the onion and cook for 5 minutes. Return the meat to the pan with the flour, herbs, ketchup, alcohol and stock, bring to a simmer and season. Tip the mixture into a large bowl; cool.

3 Grease a 1-litre pudding basin with oil or lard. Roll out two-thirds of the pastry to a large circle and use it to line the basin. Add the filling. Roll out the remaining pastry to a circle to make the lid. Using a little water, moisten the edges, put the lid on top and crimp the edges to seal. Trim off the excess pastry.

4 Create a lid using greaseproof paper and foil. Tie securely with string. Steam in a large pan of gently simmering water for 3½–4 hours.

PER SERVING 1091 kcals, protein 47g, carbs 81g, fat 60g, sat fat 29g, fibre 5g, sugar 8g, salt 2.7g

Pot-roast veal with carrots & orange

British rose veal is now available in supermarkets and from butchers. The animals are bred humanely, and the meat has a far superior flavour to most European veal.

TAKES 2 HOURS 50 MINUTES

● **SERVES 6**

1.5kg/3lb piece rolled and tied veal
  shoulder
3 garlic cloves, 1 finely sliced, 2 bashed
bunch thyme
1 tbsp olive oil
25g/1oz butter
800g/1lb 12oz new-season bunch
  carrots, trimmed, stalks still attached
1 large shallot, roughly chopped
sprinkling icing sugar
zest 1 orange, ½ pared into strips,
  ½ finely grated
150ml/¼ pint white wine
350ml/12fl oz chicken stock

1 Heat oven to 180C/160C fan/gas 4. Stud the gaps in the veal joint with the sliced garlic and some thyme. Season.
2 Heat oil and butter in a flameproof casserole dish and slowly sizzle the veal for 15 minutes, until brown all over. Remove the joint to a plate and add the carrots, shallot and icing sugar. Cook for 5 minutes until slightly caramelised. Lift out and reserve the carrots, leaving everything else in the dish. Add the rest of the thyme, the bashed garlic and the pared orange zest. Nestle the veal in the dish, then pour over the wine and stock. Cover, then put in the oven for 1 hour.
3 Remove the dish from the oven and scatter the carrots around the meat with the grated zest. Return to the oven for 1 hour, uncovered. Cook until the meat is very tender, then leave to cool slightly. Lift the meat on to a board and carve into slices. Serve with the juices from the dish and the tender carrots.

PER SERVING 425 kcals, protein 44g, carbs 10g, fat 20g, sat fat 8g, fibre 5g, sugar 9g, salt 0.8g

Roast rib of beef

A rib of beef has to be the king of all roasts. It makes a dramatic centrepiece to any Sunday lunch and is perfect served with roast spuds, greens and Yorkshire puddings.

TAKES 2½ HOURS, PLUS MARINATING OVERNIGHT ● SERVES 8

3.5kg/7½1b fore rib beef, bone in (28-day dry matured)
4 carrots
3 celery sticks
1 garlic bulb

FOR THE MARINADE

1 tbsp juniper berries
1 tbsp black peppercorns
3 rosemary sprigs, leaves picked
10 thyme sprigs, leaves picked
4 bay leaves
2 tbsp Maldon sea salt
6 tbsp rapeseed oil
2 tbsp honey

1 Toast the juniper berries in a dry pan then grind in a pestle and mortar with the black peppercorns until they begin to release their aromas. Roughly chop the rosemary and thyme leaves with the bay leaves. Add to the pestle and mortar along with the salt, oil and honey, and mix well.

2 Score the fat of the beef in a criss-cross. Rub the marinade all over the meat, massaging well. Leave overnight in the fridge. Before cooking, take it out for 1 hour so it comes to room temperature.

3 Heat oven to 200C/180C fan/gas 6. Arrange the carrots and celery in a roasting tin. Slice the garlic bulb in half and add to the tin, then put the meat on top of the vegetables. Roast in the oven for 1¾ hours, covering with foil if the meat starts to become too brown. Leave to rest covered with foil for 20 minutes before carving. Serve with the juice from the pan.

PER SERVING 841 kcals, protein 472, carbs 8g, fat 58g, sat fat 23g, fibre 2g, sugar 7g, salt 4.1g

Rosemary roast-chicken thighs, new potatoes, asparagus & garlic

Make the most of delicious new potatoes and asparagus when they are at their best between April and May. This is a perfect spring supper for four.

TAKES 55 MINUTES • SERVES 4

750g/1lb 10oz new potatoes (preferably Jersey Royals), halved
2 large bunches asparagus, woody ends discarded
1 whole garlic bulb, cloves separated
1 tbsp olive oil
1 lemon, halved
small handful rosemary sprigs
8 chicken thighs

1 Heat oven to 200C/180C fan/gas 6. Put the potatoes, asparagus, garlic cloves, oil and lots of seasoning in a large roasting dish (about 30 x 20cm). Squeeze over all the juice from the lemon halves, then cut them into chunks and add them to the dish. Toss everything together, cover the dish with foil and roast for about 15 minutes.

2 Remove the foil and mix through the rosemary. Season the chicken thighs and arrange in the dish.

3 Roast for another 25–30 minutes until the potatoes are tender and the chicken is crisp and cooked through. Serve the dish in the middle of the table for everyone to dig in.

PER SERVING 509 kcals, protein 39g, carbs 32g, fat 24g, sat fat 6g, fibre 6g, sugar 5g, salt 0.3g

Sweet-spiced lamb shanks with quince

Quince are in season between September and early November, and although not readily available in supermarkets, they can be found in many farmers' markets.

TAKES 3 HOURS 10 MINUTES

● **SERVES 4**

1 tbsp olive oil

4 lamb shanks

large knob butter

2 large onions, halved then cut into wedges

4 garlic cloves, crushed

4 strips zest from 1 unwaxed lemon, plus the juice

2 tsp ground cinnamon

2 tsp ground coriander

1 tsp ground ginger

1 tsp ground cumin

good pinch saffron strands (optional)

1 heaped tbsp tomato purée

1 tbsp clear honey

400ml/14fl oz good lamb or beef stock

2 quinces, peeled, quartered and cored

1 Heat the oil in a large frying pan. Season the shanks, then brown in the oil for 10 minutes, or until dark golden all over.

2 Meanwhile, in a casserole dish or large pan with a lid, melt the butter. Soften the onions for 10 minutes on a medium heat until golden, then add the garlic. Heat oven to 160C/140C fan/gas 3.

3 Add the strips of lemon zest and spices to the onion pan. Cook for 1 minute, then stir in the tomato purée, honey, stock and half the lemon juice. Sit the shanks in the pan, then poke the quince quarters in and around the meat. (It might be quite a tight fit, but the meat will shrink as it cooks.) Bring to a simmer, then cover with a lid and braise in the oven for 2 hours.

4 Remove the lid and cook for 30 minutes more. Spoon away any excess fat. Season, add the remaining lemon juice and serve the sauce with the lamb.

PER SERVING 624 kcals, protein 59g, carbs 14g, fat 36g, sat fat 16g, fibre 2g, sugar 11g, salt 0.4g

One-pot pork with bay, olives & orange

This dish can all be cooked in one pan, saving you some washing up! Serve in shallow bowls with chunks of crusty bread to mop up the sauce.

TAKES 3¼ HOURS ● **SERVES 6**

85g/3oz sundried tomatoes in oil, roughly chopped, plus 2–3 tbsp oil from the jar

1kg/2lb 4oz pork shoulders, cut into chunky cubes

2 tbsp plain flour, seasoned

400g/14oz shallots, peeled

1 onion, thinly sliced

3 bay leaves

few thyme sprigs

5 garlic cloves, thinly sliced

400ml/14fl oz red wine

strip zest and juice 1 orange

350ml/12fl oz chicken stock

400g can chopped plum tomatoes

800g/1lb 12oz large new potatoes, peeled and halved or cut into fat slices, depending on size

70g pack dry black olives

1 Heat 1 tablespoon of the sundried tomato oil in a large, flameproof casserole dish. Toss the pork in the flour, then brown it in two batches, transferring to a large bowl once golden and crusted.

2 Tip 1 tablespoon of the tomato oil, the shallots, onion, bay leaves and thyme into the pan and fry for 5 minutes until golden. Stir in the garlic and sundried tomatoes, cook for 1 minute more, then tip on to the pork.

3 Splash the wine and orange juice into the dish, add the orange zest and boil for 5 minutes. Add the meat and onions

4 When ready to cook, heat oven to 160C/140C fan/gas 3. Stir the stock, canned tomatoes, potatoes and olives into the casserole, then bring to a simmer. Prod the potatoes far under the surface of the liquid. Cover, then cook in the oven for 2½ hours. Spoon away any excess fat and let the stew rest briefly before serving.

PER SERVING 670 kcals, protein 37g, carbs 35g, fat 36g, sat fat 11g, fibre 7g, sugar 9g, salt 1.2g

Braised lamb & two-potato dauphinoise pie

This hearty pie combines two comfort-food classics: lamb hotpot and potato dauphinoise. Delicious served with Savoy cabbage and peas.

TAKES 3 HOURS 50 MINUTES

● **SERVES 8**

3 large carrots, cut into large chunks
1 onion, roughly chopped
1 bulb garlic, split in 2
few sprigs each rosemary and thyme
2 bay leaves
1 tbsp tomato purée
1 shoulder of lamb on the bone (about 2.5kg/5lb 8oz)
1 x 75cl bottle red wine

FOR THE TOPPING

4–5 potatoes, sliced into rounds
4 sweet potatoes, sliced into rounds
150ml/¼ pint double cream
few knobs butter

1 Heat oven to 180C/160C fan/gas 4. Scatter the veg and herbs in a large ovenproof dish, and stir in the tomato purée. Sit the lamb on top, pour over the wine and season. Cover the pan, bring to a simmer on the stove then cook in the oven for 3 hours. Remove from the oven, cool, then chill overnight.

2 Remove the hard fat from around the lamb. Lift the lamb out of the tin, keeping any jellified juices. Shred the meat, discarding any fat and the bones. Place the lamb, jellified stock and vegetables in a pie dish. Set aside.

3 Heat oven to 200C/180C fan/gas 6. Make the topping. Hard-boil the potato slices in a pan of water for 3 minutes and drain. Tip back into the pan, add most of the cream and season. Arrange the potatoes in circles on top of the meat and veg. Drizzle with the remaining cream and dot with butter. Bake for 40 minutes–1 hour, until golden.

PER SERVING 645 kcals, protein 49g, carbs 24g, fat 32g, sat fat 17g, fibre 3g, sugar 9g, salt 0.6g

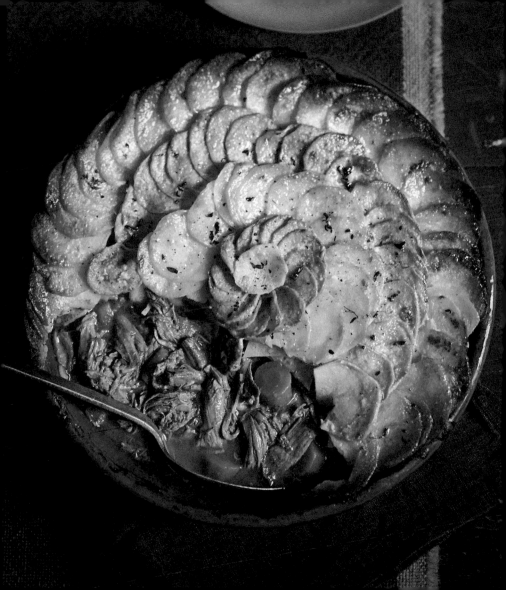

Roast beef with chilli, pine nut & parsley dressing

Give your roast a makeover by serving on a platter drizzled with a punchy dressing.

TAKES 1 HOUR 10 MINUTES
- **SERVES 10–12**

2kg/4lb 8oz beef sirloin joint
3 red chillies
5 garlic cloves
few thyme sprigs or 1 tsp dried thyme
8 tbsp olive oil
50g/2oz pine nuts
1 tsp Dijon mustard
2 tbsp sherry vinegar
good handful parsley leaves, roughly
 chopped

1 Heat oven to 180C/160C fan/gas 4. Wipe the meat with kitchen paper and set, fat-side down, in a roasting tin. Finely chop 2 chillies, 3 garlic cloves and the thyme. Mix with 3 tablespoons of the oil, season, then rub over the meat. Turn the meat fat-side up and rub in the remaining flavoured oil. Roast the joint for 40–50 minutes for medium-rare, 60–65 minutes for medium.

2 Lightly toast the pine nuts in a frying pan, then tip into a bowl. Heat 1 tablespoon of the oil in the pan, thinly slice the remaining garlic and fry until browned. Tip into a separate bowl. Finely chop the remaining chilli and whisk in the bowl with the mustard and vinegar. Whisk in the remaining oil and half the chopped parsley.

3 Rest the meat for 20 minutes. Arrange over a platter in thin slices. Spoon over a little dressing, and scatter with the pine nuts and the rest of the parsley. Serve the remaining dressing separately.

PER SERVING (10) 427 kcals, protein 40g, carbs 1g, fat 29g, sat fat 9g, fibre none, sugar none, salt 0.2g

Slow-cooked duck legs in port

This treat for two can easily be doubled, tripled or quadrupled, depending on how many guests you're feeding. Serve with a creamy potato gratin and your favourite veg.

TAKES 2¾ HOURS • **SERVES 2**

2 duck legs
2 carrots, roughly chopped
1 small onion, roughly chopped
1 tbsp plain flour
1 bay leaf
1 star anise
2 whole cloves
2 strips orange skin (with a potato peeler)
150ml/¼ pint port
500ml/18fl oz chicken stock

1 Heat oven to 160C/140C fan/gas 3. Put the duck legs in a flameproof casserole set over a medium heat. Brown all over, then remove from the casserole and set aside. Pour off all but 1 tablespoon of the fat, leaving more in the pan if you are doubling or tripling the recipe. Add the carrots and onion to the casserole, and cook for 5–10 minutes or until starting to caramelise. Stir in the flour and cook for 1 minute more. Return the duck to the pan along with the remaining ingredients. Bring to a simmer, then cover with a lid and put in the oven for 2 hours.
2 Remove the casserole from the oven. Scoop the duck legs from the cooking liquid, then strain the liquid into a clean pan and bring to a rapid boil. Reduce the sauce by half until thickened and glossy. Add the duck legs and heat through. Serve straight away, or chill for up to 2 days and reheat before serving.

PER SERVING 532 kcals, protein 44g, carbs 28g, fat 18g, sat fat 4g, fibre 4g, sugar 18g, salt 1g

Bacon- & spinach-wrapped beef Wellington

Impress your guests with a dinner-party favourite; it may look like a challenge, but this recipe is sure to give you perfect results every time!

TAKES 1 HOUR, PLUS CHILLING
● **SERVES 6**

large knob butter
1 tbsp sunflower oil
700–800g/1lb 9oz–1lb 12oz beef fillet cut from the centre of the fillet so it's all the same size
12 thin slices smoked pancetta or rindless streaky bacon
500g/1lb 2oz spinach leaves, cooked, water squeezed out
flour, for dusting
500g pack all-butter puff pastry, rolled to a 30 x 40cm rectangle
2 egg yolks
flaky sea salt, for sprinkling

1 Heat the butter and oil in a pan, brown the fillet on all sides, then set aside. Lay a large sheet of cling film on your work surface. Overlap the pancetta or bacon slices on it in a row, then scatter over the spinach. Sit the beef on top. Using the edge of the cling film, lift and roll the pancetta and spinach to encase the beef. Then roll everything into a tight sausage.

2 Lightly brush the pastry all over with the egg yolk. Carefully remove the cling film from the prosciutto parcel and lay in the middle of the pastry. Fold the shorter edges over the fillet then roll the whole thing around the fillet to encase. Chill for at least 30 minutes or up to 1 day.

3 Heat oven to 220C/200C fan/gas 7 with a baking tray in it. Transfer the Wellington to the tray, sealed-side down, and brush with yolk. Bake for 10 minutes, then reduce the oven to 200C/180C fan/gas 6 and bake for 30 minutes for medium-rare, 35 minutes for medium and about 45 minutes for well done.

PER SERVING 596 kcals, protein 37g, carbs 31g, fat 37g, sat fat 16g, fibre 2g, sugar 2g, salt 1.6g

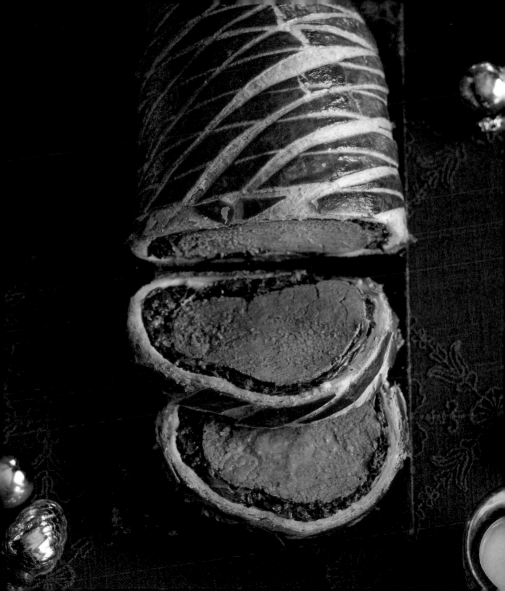

Winter greens with bacon butter

Make a roll of bacon-flavoured butter to keep in the fridge or freezer to enhance
simply cooked spinach, kale, peas or spring greens.

TAKES 35 MINUTES ● SERVES 6, WITH
LEFTOVER BUTTER
6 rashers smoked streaky bacon
140g/5oz salted butter, softened
400g/14oz kale or other winter greens

1 Heat grill on a medium–high setting. Cook the bacon under the grill, turning halfway through cooking, until really crisp. Remove from under the grill, drain on kitchen paper and leave to cool completely.
2 Put the bacon in a food processor and whizz until finely chopped. Add the butter and some black pepper, and blend again until combined. You can now either put the bacon butter in a dish or roll in cling film and chill for up to 3 days, or freeze for up to 2 months.
3 Bring a large pan of salted water to the boil. Add the kale and cook for 3–4 minutes until tender. Drain well, top with half of the butter, and toss to help it melt and coat the kale.

PER SERVING 136 kcals, protein 4g, carbs 1g, fat 13g, sat fat 7g, fibre 3g, sugar 1g, salt 0.8g

Sticky liquorice carrots

This might sound like an unusual flavour combination, but it works really well served with beef or venison.

TAKES 15 MINUTES • SERVES 6

50g/2oz soft black liquorice
50g/2oz salted butter
800g/1lb 2oz carrots, peeled and cut
    into batons

1 Chop the liquorice very finely and put in a small pan with about 5cm/2in water. Boil, topping up with water to keep the liquorice covered at all times, mashing and stirring occasionally, until nearly all the lumps of liquorice have disappeared and you're left with black, syrupy liquorice water. Strain into a new pan, add the butter and gently bubble until you have a consistency between runny honey and gravy. You can make this ahead and reheat in a microwave to melt, if you like.

2 Boil a big pan of water. Add the carrots and cook for a couple of minutes, until just tender. Drain well, then tip back into the pan with the hot liquorice syrup. Toss together to coat, season and tip into a dish to serve.

PER SERVING 117 kcals, protein 1g, carbs 11g, fat 8g, sat fat 5g, fibre 5g, sugar 9g, salt 0.3g

Brown-butter-basted radishes

Radishes aren't just for slicing into salads. Try cooking them in nutty brown butter to release their peppery flavour.

TAKES 25 MINUTES ● SERVES 4
85g/3oz butter
600g/1lb 4oz radishes, leaves trimmed
juice ½ lemon
sea salt, to taste

1 Put half the butter in a heavy-based frying pan that will fit all the radishes snugly. Heat the butter until it's just foaming and starting to turn a nut-brown, then add the radishes and turn to coat in the butter.

2 Fry the radishes, turning them every few minutes and adding small knobs of the remaining butter as they cook, for 10 minutes until they're glazed and have softened and wrinkled. Turn the heat up to maximum, add the lemon juice, let it sizzle for 1 minute, then remove the pan from the heat. Season with sea salt and serve.

PER SERVING 176 kcals, protein 1g, carbs 3g, fat 18g, sat fat 11g, fibre 2g, sugar 3g, salt 0.4g

Spring greens, fennel & apples

Use sharp green eating apples for this recipe, as they will keep their shape on cooking and give a nice bite to the dish.

TAKES 15 MINUTES ● SERVES 6

2 tbsp olive oil

1 large head spring greens, finely shredded

1 fennel bulb, finely sliced (reserve the fronds)

2 green apples, finely sliced or cut into matchsticks

juice ½ lemon

1 Heat the oil in a wok or a large pan. Add the spring greens, fennel and apples, then season and stir-fry for 2–3 minutes to wilt the veg. Add the lemon juice and cook for 1 minute more until everything is cooked but still has a nice bite.

2 Sprinkle with the reserved fennel fronds and serve straight away.

PER SERVING 102 kcals, protein 4g, carbs 9g, fat 5g, sat fat 1g, fibre 8g, sugar 7g, salt 0.1g

Herby fondant potatoes

This classic method of cooking potatoes in stock results in really tasty potatoes with golden, caramelised edges.

TAKES 1 HOUR 25 MINUTES
● **SERVES 6**

1.5kg/3lb small floury potatoes, like Desirée or Maris Piper, peeled
4 tbsp olive oil
3 garlic cloves, bashed
3 thyme sprigs
3 lemon thyme sprigs
2 rosemary sprigs
3 bay leaves
pared zest 1 lemon, peeled with a vegetable peeler
about 600ml/1 pint chicken or vegetable stock

1 Trim the tops and bottoms of the potatoes so that they lie flat on both sides. Heat the oil in a large frying pan or flameproof casserole and fry for about 10–15 minutes until dark golden.

2 Poke in the garlic, thymes, rosemary, bay leaves and zest, then pour in enough stock to go halfway up the side of the potatoes. Simmer for 20–30 minutes, then turn the potatoes and cook for a further 20–30 minutes, topping up with more stock if it evaporates. Continue cooking until the potatoes are really tender and most of the stock has gone. Season well and serve.

PER SERVING 272 kcals, protein 9g, carbs 41g, fat 8g, sat fat 1g, fibre 4g, sugar 2g, salt 0.3g

Roasted sprouts with chestnuts & bacon

Make more of the humble sprout by combining it with sizzled crispy bacon and nutty chestnuts.

TAKES 45 MINUTES ● SERVES 8

1.5kg/3lb Brussels sprouts, trimmed
200g vacuum-pack whole chestnuts, roughly chopped in half
200g/7oz smoked bacon lardons
1 tsp vegetable oil

1 Heat oven to 220C/200C fan/gas 7. Bring a large pan of water to the boil, add the sprouts and cook for 5 minutes. Drain and refresh in cold water.

2 Toss the sprouts with all the other ingredients in a bowl and season with a pinch of salt and a good grinding of black pepper. Tip on to a large baking tray in a single layer. Put in the oven and roast for 30 minutes, tossing halfway through, until the bacon is crispy and the sprouts are golden and tender.

PER SERVING 188 kcals, protein 12g, carbs 16g, fat 8g, sat fat 3g, fibre 9g, sugar 7g, salt 0.7g

Salted-caramel parsnips

Transform roasted parsnips into a super special dish, with a coating of salted caramel.

TAKES 45 MINUTES • SERVES 6

1kg/2lb 4oz parsnips, peeled
3 tbsp rapeseed oil
50g/2oz caster sugar
large knob butter
1 tsp sea salt

1 Heat oven to 220C/200C fan/gas 7. Halve the parsnips, then cut the thicker end in two lengthways. Boil for 5 minutes, drain and steam-dry for a few minutes. Meanwhile, pour the oil into a roasting tin and heat in the oven for 3 minutes.

2 Remove the tin from the oven and add the parsnips to the hot oil, turning them to coat. Roast for 30–35 minutes, turning them over halfway through, until golden and crisp.

3 With 10 minutes to go, tip the sugar and 2 tablespoons water into a small frying pan. Heat gently until the sugar has dissolved. Turn up the heat and bring it to a boil. Swirl the pan around until the sugar reaches a caramel colour, then remove from the heat. Stand well back and add 3½ tablespoons cold water. Return to the heat, add the butter and salt, and stir. Add a splash more water if it isn't runny. Drizzle the salted caramel over the parsnips to serve.

PER SERVING 205 kcals, protein 3g, carbs 29g, fat 9g, sat fat 2g, fibre 8g, sugar 18g, salt 1.4g

Layered squash, barley & spinach pie

A hearty pie, perfect for a wintry Sunday lunch.

TAKES 3 HOURS 20 MINUTES

● **SERVES 8**

1 small butternut squash (about 1kg/
   2lb 4oz), peeled, cubed, roasted until
   tender then cooled
3 tbsp olive oil, plus extra for brushing
3 onions, finely chopped
3 garlic cloves, crushed
100g/4oz mushrooms, sliced
85g/3oz cooked chestnuts, quartered
100g/4oz pearl barley
1.2 litres/2 pints vegetable stock
1 tbsp dark soy sauce
zest 1 lemon
250g tub ricotta
200g/7oz full-fat soft cheese
handful sage, leaves chopped
400g/14oz spinach, cooked and water
   squeezed out, then roughly chopped
bunch parsley, leaves chopped

FOR THE PASTRY
700g/1lb 9oz plain flour
140g/5oz butter
85g/3oz white vegetable shortening
100ml/3½fl oz milk
1 egg, lightly beaten
few bay leaves (optional)

1 Heat the oil in a pan and cook the onions and garlic for 10 minutes. Remove two-thirds then add the mushrooms, chestnuts, barley, stock and soy. Bubble for 30 minutes until the barley is tender.
2 Stir the zest and cheeses into the reserved onions. Mix a third with the sage and squash then mix spinach and parsley into the rest. Oil a 900g loaf tin.
3 Tip the flour and 2 teaspoons salt into a bowl. Heat the butter, shortening, milk and 200ml/7fl oz water in a pan. Once melted, tip on to the flour and beat with a wooden spoon until combined. Knead until smooth. Set aside a third and roll the rest into a rectangle to line the tin.
4 Once lined, add the fillings in layers, finishing with squash. Roll out the remaining pastry, brush with egg, then lift the lid over the top and crimp to seal. Brush with egg and chill for 1 hour.
5 Heat oven to 200C/180C fan/gas 6. Bake for 30 minutes; then for 1½ hours at 180C/160C fan/gas 4.

PER SERVING 889 kcals protein 19g, carbs 99g, fat 49g, sat fat 24g, fibre none, sugar 13g, salt 1.31g

Squash & blue-cheese Wellington

This stunning centrepiece works well with all the traditional roast accompaniments.

TAKES 45 MINUTES, PLUS CHILLING
● **SERVES 6**

850g/1lb 14oz solid piece from the long end of a large butternut squash, peeled and cut lengthways into 8 long pieces (you may need to use the ends of 2 squashes)

400g pack shallots, peeled and halved if large

2 tbsp olive oil

50g/2oz pecan nuts

1½ tbsp maple syrup

1½ tbsp balsamic vinegar

500g pack all-butter puff pastry

plain flour, for dusting

1 tbsp chopped sage leaves

200g/7oz blue Wensleydale cheese, diced

1 egg, beaten, to glaze

1 Heat oven to 200C/180C fan/gas 6. Toss the squash and shallots in oil in a roasting tin. Season and roast for 20 minutes. Add the pecans and roast for 10 minutes. Cool.

2 Transfer the nuts and shallots to a pan, with the syrup and vinegar. Stir over heat until the shallots start to caramelise. Cool.

3 Roll out the pastry on a floured surface to 32 x 38cm. Trim 2cm/¾in from one long edge and set aside. Transfer to a baking tray. Place half the squash in the middle of the longest length to make a rectangle, keeping a border of pastry all around. Put 2 pieces of squash on top. Trim the remaining squash and put crossways at the end. Scatter over the sage and cheese, then the shallots mix. Lightly press to compact.

4 Brush the pastry edges with some egg, then draw the two long edges up and pinch to seal. Tuck the pastry under at both ends then brush with more egg. Decorate with leaf shapes from the pastry trimmings. Glaze and make two air holes.

5 Chill for at least 30 minutes. Bake for 30–40 minutes, then rest for 10 minutes.

PER SERVING 623 kcals, protein 17g, carbs 47g, fat 41g, sat fat 17g, fibre 5g, sugar 13g, salt 1.2g

Shallot Tatin

Sweet, caramelised shallots are the star of this veggie main. Make sure you take the caramel to a nice rich golden colour for the best flavour.

TAKES 1 HOUR • SERVES 4

450g/1lb shallots
3 tbsp demerara sugar
50g/2oz butter
1 tsp thyme leaves
1 tbsp balsamic vinegar
a few grindings of cracked black
   pepper
plain flour, for dusting
500g pack puff pastry
rocket leaves and goat's cheese salad,
   to serve

1 Heat oven to 200C/180C fan/gas 6. Pour boiling water over the shallots and leave them until the water cools. (This makes it easier to slip the skins off.) Peel and halve the shallots, then set aside. Put the sugar in a 23cm-round ovenproof frying pan and heat until it dissolves and you have a sticky caramel. Add the butter, thyme, a splash of balsamic vinegar and cracked black pepper – take care as the vinegar will spit.

2 Remove the pan from the heat and put all the shallots into the pan, cut-side down. On a lightly floured surface, roll out the pastry and cut out a round 2cm/¾in larger than the pan. Drape the pastry over the shallots and tuck in the edges, so that it 'hugs' the shallots. Place the pan in the oven and cook for 25–30 minutes until the pastry is puffed up and golden. Leave to rest for 1 minute, then invert the tart on to a plate. Serve with a punchy salad of rocket and goat's cheese.

PER SERVING 649 kcals, protein 9g, carbs 63g, fat 40g, sat fat 21g, fibre 2g, sugar 21g, salt 1.2g

Parsnip, cranberry & chestnut loaf

This parsnip nut loaf makes an excellent main for Christmas lunch, but also doubles up as extra stuffing for the turkey-loving guests.

TAKES 2 HOURS • SERVES 4–6

4 tbsp butter, plus a little extra for greasing
3 onions, chopped
15g pack sage, 6 leaves reserved, rest shredded
200g vac-packed cooked whole chestnuts, finely chopped
100g/4oz walnuts, finely chopped
100g/4oz breadcrumbs
½ tsp ground mace
1 egg, beaten
500g/1lb 2oz cranberries
175g/6oz caster sugar
550g/1lb 4oz parsnips, choose long, thin ones, if you can, peeled then halved lengthways
1 tbsp honey

1 Melt 1 tablespoon of the butter in a pan, cook the onions and sage for 10–15 minutes until soft. Tip into a bowl and cool. Add the chestnuts, walnuts, breadcrumbs, mace, egg, 1 teaspoon salt and some pepper, and mix well.

2 Tip the cranberries and sugar into a pan and simmer for 8–10 minutes until sticky, then cool. Grease a 900g loaf tin, line with baking parchment, then grease this too.

3 Boil the parsnips for 3½ minutes; drain. Cut off lengths of parsnip to fit widthways across the bottom of your tin, enough to line the entire base. Roughly chop leftover parsnip and stir into the nut mix.

4 Heat oven to 180C/160C fan/gas 4. Mix the parsnip lengths with remaining butter and honey, then fit them into the tin. Top with half the nut mix. Spread half the cranberry sauce on top. Top with the remaining nut mix. Cover with foil then bake for 1 hour. Serve sliced with the remaining cranberry sauce.

PER SERVING (6) 819 kcals, protein 14g, carbs 117g, fat 36g, sat fat 11g, fibre 15g, sugar 71g, salt 0.86g

Squash & sage pithivier

This pie is an individual serving, but the recipe can be easily doubled.

TAKES 50 MINUTES • SERVES 1

¼ x 500g pack puff pastry
flour, for dusting
1 tsp wholegrain mustard
4 tbsp mascarpone
1 tbsp breadcrumbs, fresh or dried
6 sage leaves, chopped, plus a few
    extra to garnish
1 garlic clove, finely grated to a paste
½ the top end of a butternut squash
    (about 250g/9oz), thinly sliced into
    rounds
1 egg, beaten

1 Heat oven to 200C/180C fan/gas 6. Halve the pastry piece, with one half slightly bigger. Roll out the smaller half on a floured surface to a circle 15cm/6in in diameter. Spread over the mustard, 2cm/¾in in from the edge. Mix together the mascarpone, breadcrumbs, chopped sage and the garlic, and season.

2 Arrange a few squash slices, overlapping, to cover the mustard. Spread with some of the mascarpone mixture. Repeat, making smaller circles with the squash each time, and spreading mascarpone between each layer until the top is just one slice of squash and you have made a rough dome shape.

3 Thinly roll out the remaining pastry. Use to cover the squash dome. Press the pastry edges to seal. Brush with the egg, then poke a steam hole in the top. Dip a few sage leaves in the remaining egg and stick on top. Bake on a baking sheet for 35–40 minutes until a skewer poked through the hole goes through the veg easily.

PER SERVING 1022 kcals, protein 21g, carbs 76g, fat 72g, sat fat 37g, fibre 7g, sugar 16g, salt 2.1g

Crisp spinach tart with squash wedges

A tart lined with filo pastry makes a lighter alternative to shortcrust or puff pastry. This veggie tart is served with wedges of roasted butternut squash.

TAKES 1 HOUR • SERVES 4

3 eggs, beaten
250g tub ricotta
200g/7oz frozen leaf spinach, defrosted, squeezed dry and chopped
1 spring onion, finely sliced
½ x 145g tub fresh basil pesto
1 butternut squash, peeled and cut into wedges
½ x 240g pack Sun-blushed tomatoes in oil, roughly chopped, oil drained and reserved
270g pack filo pastry
knob butter, melted

1 Mix together the eggs and ricotta, then add the spinach, spring onion and pesto. Set aside.

2 Heat oven to 180C/160C fan/gas 4. Toss the squash in a little of the tomato oil, spread out on a baking sheet and roast for 15 minutes. Unwrap the pastry and cover with a just damp piece of kitchen paper. Mix the butter with 2 tablespoons of the tomato oil.

3 Brush the butter mixture over 1 sheet of the pastry, then place in a 23cm-round tart tin. Brush another piece of pastry with butter and put slightly further around the tin. Keep brushing and lining the tin until you have used up the pastry and the tin is covered. Trim off any pastry overhanging the edges, then bake for 5–10 minutes until starting to crisp. Spoon the spinach mixture into the tin and scatter with the tomatoes. Cook for 20–25 minutes alongside the squash until set and the squash cooked through.

PER SERVING 645 kcals, protein 24g, carbs 64g, fat 34g, sat fat 10g, fibre 6g, sugar 17g, salt 2.8g

Winter vegetable pie

This pie is a great way to use up leftovers lurking in your vegetable drawer.

TAKES 1 HOUR ● SERVES 4

2 tbsp olive oil
2 onions, sliced
1 tbsp flour
300g/11oz (about 2 large) carrots, cut into small batons
½ cauliflower, broken into small florets
4 garlic cloves, finely sliced
1 rosemary sprig, leaves finely chopped
400g can chopped tomatoes
200g/7oz frozen peas
900g/2lb potatoes, cut into chunks
up to 200ml/7fl oz milk

1 Heat 1 tablespoon of the oil in a flameproof dish over a medium heat. Add the onions and cook for 10 minutes until softened, then stir in the flour and cook for 2 minutes. Add the carrots, cauliflower, garlic and rosemary. Cook for 5 minutes, stirring, until they soften.

2 Tip the tomatoes and a can of water into the vegetables. Simmer, covered, for 10 minutes, then cook, uncovered, for 10–15 minutes, until the sauce has thickened and the veg is cooked. Season, stir in the peas and cook for 1 minute.

3 Meanwhile, in a separate pan, boil the potatoes for 10–15 minutes until tender. Drain, then put back in the pan and mash. Stir through enough milk to reach a fairly soft consistency, then add the remaining olive oil and season.

4 Heat the grill. Spoon the hot vegetable mix into a pie dish, top with the mash and drag a fork lightly over the surface. Place under the grill for a few minutes until the top is crisp golden brown.

PER SERVING 388 kcals, protein 15g, carbs 62g, fat 8g, sat fat 2g, fibre 11g, sugar 18g, salt 0.3g

Parsnip pilaf

Make parsnips the star of the show with this Middle-Eastern-flavoured pilaf.

TAKES 1 HOUR 35 MINUTES ● SERVES 8

1 vegetable stock cube

300g/11oz basmati rice, soaked and
   rinsed

140g/5oz red split lentils

1kg/2lb 4oz parsnips, 200g/7oz grated,
   remainder cut into long chunky
   wedges

4 tbsp olive oil

zest 2 oranges (use the juice in the
   sauce)

2 tsp cumin seeds

2 tbsp honey

3 onions, sliced

1 tsp each turmeric powder, ground
   coriander and caraway

100g/4oz raisins

zest 3 lemons (use the juice in the
   sauce)

25g/1oz butter

FOR THE HERB SAUCE

25g/1oz pistachio nuts

juice 3 lemons

juice 2 oranges

small bunch coriander

small bunch each dill, parsley and mint,
   stalks discarded

1 Heat oven to 200C/180C fan/gas 6.
Boil a pan of water with the stock cube
in it. Add the rice and lentils, and simmer
for 5 minutes until starting to soften. Drain.

2 Toss the chunky parsnips with half the
oil, the orange zest, half the cumin seeds
and some seasoning in a roasting tin.
Roast for 30 minutes until golden. Drizzle
with honey and roast for 5–10 minutes.

3 Heat 1 tablespoon of the oil in a wide
flameproof dish. Fry the onions until
browned. Stir in the rest of the spices
and cumin, and cook for 1 minute. Add
the grated parsnips and raisins, and
cook for 1 minute. Turn down the heat .
Stir in the rice mix and lemon zest.

4 Melt the butter and remaining oil in a
pan. Tip in the rice mixture and flatten.
Poke 3 steam holes in the rice. Cover the
pan with a tea towel, then put on the lid.
Cook for 20–25 minutes on a low heat.

5 Whizz the sauce ingredients to a
salsa-like mix. Spread the rice on a
platter. Top with the parsnips and sauce.

PER SERVING 326 kcals, protein 7g, carbs 52g,
fat 9g, sat fat 2g, fibre 8g, sugar 20g, salt 0.4g

Veg & cheesy-rice bake

Make the most of a glut of courgettes, tomatoes and aubergines in late summer with this delicious risotto-topped bake.

TAKES 1 HOUR 20 MINUTES
- **SERVES 4**

1 onion, chopped
1 tbsp olive oil
2 courgettes, sliced
1 aubergine, diced
450g/1lb fresh tomatoes, chopped (or
   400g can chopped tomatoes)
200g/7oz risotto rice
2 eggs, beaten
140g/5oz Cheddar, grated

1 Sweat the onion in the oil for 10 minutes, until soft and lightly golden. Add the courgettes and aubergine. Fry until golden brown. Add the tomatoes and some seasoning, then cover and simmer for 30 minutes, uncovering for the final 15 minutes if using fresh tomatoes. Heat oven to 200C/180C fan/ gas 6.

2 Meanwhile, cook the rice in a large pot of salted boiling water for 20 minutes or until tender. Drain and mix with the eggs and two-thirds of the cheese.

3 Put the courgette-and-tomato mix in an ovenproof dish. Spoon the rice mixture over and smooth it out. Sprinkle over the rest of the cheese. Bake for 30 minutes until bubbling and golden.

PER SERVING 443 kcals, protein 20g, carbs 48g, fat 19g, sat 9g, fibre 6g, sugar 8g, salt 0.8g

Crunchy baked tomato & onion gratin

A-low-on-cost, but full-on-flavour dish. For best results, make throughout the summer months when tomatoes are at their best.

TAKES 1¾ HOURS • SERVES 6

4 tbsp olive oil
3 onions, thinly sliced
3 garlic cloves, thinly sliced
1.2kg/2lb 10oz mixed tomatoes, from really big to cherry size
8 thyme or oregano sprigs, or a mixture, stripped, plus a few more
1 tbsp golden caster sugar
50–85g/2–3oz fresh white breadcrumbs (if you've got a crust, use this so the crumbs are nice and golden)

1 Heat oven to 180C/160C fan/gas 4. Heat half the oil in a pan and gently soften the onions and garlic for 15–20 minutes until really soft and sticky but not browned. Put the garlicky onions, tomatoes (halve the large ones), herbs, sugar and breadcrumbs in a baking dish, season well and toss together.

2 Drizzle with the remaining oil, scatter with a few more herb sprigs and bake for 1 hour until going golden on top and the tomatoes are juicy.

PER SERVING 189 kcals, protein 4g, carbs 24g, fat 8g, sat fat 1g, fibre 3g, sugar 13g, salt 0.3g

Butter pie with apples & cheese

This hearty potato pie hails from Lancashire and is a little like a giant cheese pasty.

TAKES 1 HOUR 50 MINUTES ● CUTS INTO 10 SLICES

50g/2oz unsalted butter
2 large onions, halved and thinly sliced
½ small pack thyme
2 Cox's apples, peeled and sliced
splash lemon juice
800g/1lb 12oz potatoes (we used
    Desiree), sliced into 5mm/¼in
    rounds, cooked until tender
500g/1lb 2oz all-butter shortcrust
    pastry, defrosted if frozen
plain flour, for dusting
175g/6oz mature Lancashire cheese or
    Cheddar, grated or crumbled
beaten egg, to glaze

1 Heat the butter in a wide pan. Stir in the onions, some seasoning and the thyme, then cover and cook for 8 minutes until turning golden. Toss the apples with the lemon juice, then cook, uncovered, with the onions for 5 minutes, stirring. Mix in the potatoes. Cool. Remove the thyme.
2 Cut two-thirds of the pastry from the block then roll out on a floured surface to line a deep 23cm-round loose-bottomed tart tin. Fill the pastry case with the potato mix and all but 1 tablespoon of the cheese and season. Brush the edge of the case with some egg. Heat oven to 190C/170C fan/gas 5 and put a baking tray in the oven to heat.
3 Roll the remaining pastry to cover the top of the pie. Press the edges together and trim by pressing your thumb around the rim of the tin. Brush with egg, then cut slits to allow steam to escape. Slide the pie on to the hot baking sheet and cook for 1 hour, scattering with the remaining cheese with 10 minutes to go, until the pastry and cheese are golden.

PER SLICE 429 kcals, protein 9g, carbs 39g, fat 26g, sat fat 12g, fibre 4g, sugar 5g, salt 0.9g

Tomato & harissa stew with Cheddar dumplings

This stew makes a nice alternative to the traditional meat-heavy version and is topped with cheesy dumplings for added comfort factor.

TAKES 55 MINUTES ● SERVES 4

1 tbsp sunflower oil

1 onion, chopped

4 celery sticks, thickly sliced

400g can plum tomatoes

1 tbsp harissa paste

2 large courgettes, halved lengthways
and thickly sliced

400g can chickpeas, drained and rinsed

1 vegetable stock cube

FOR THE DUMPLINGS

25g/1oz butter, diced

200g/7oz self-raising flour

1 tsp baking powder

75g/2½oz extra mature Cheddar, finely
grated

100ml/3½fl oz milk

1 Heat the oil in a large wide-topped casserole dish with a lid, then fry the onion and celery for 5 minutes until softening and starting to colour. Tip in the tomatoes and a can of water, then stir in the harissa, courgettes and chickpeas, and crumble in the stock cube. Cover and simmer for 20 minutes until the veg is almost tender. Heat oven to 200C/180C fan/gas 6.

2 Meanwhile, rub the butter into the flour and baking powder with a good pinch of salt, then mix in the cheese with a round-bladed knife. About 2 minutes before the stew is ready, pour the milk into the dumpling mix and stir with the knife to make a dough. Turn out on to your work surface (no need to flour it), lightly shape into a sausage and cut into eight equal pieces.

3 Put the dumplings on top of the stew and bake in the oven for 15–20 minutes until golden and cooked through.

PER SERVING 444 kcals, protein 16g, carbs 54g, fat 17g, sat fat 8g, fibre 7g, sugar 7g, salt 2.6g

Spinach, cheese & onion-rice torte

Risotto rice cooks in the filling to give this torte a lovely creamy texture.

TAKES 1 HOUR 20 MINUTES

● **SERVES 6**

400g/14oz spinach leaves, washed
1 large onion, finely chopped
2 tbsp olive oil
2 garlic cloves, finely chopped
pinch chilli flakes
300g/11oz courgettes, cubed
100g/4oz risotto rice
100g/4oz mature Cheddar, grated
500g pack shortcrust pastry
2 large eggs and 1 medium egg
1 tbsp Dijon mustard
flour, for dusting
2 tbsp milk
2 tsp sesame seeds

1 Gently heat the spinach in a pan for 1–2 minutes until wilted. Cool, squeeze out the excess water and finely chop.

2 Gently cook the onion in a frying pan in the oil for 5 minutes, until softened. Stir in the garlic and chilli flakes, and cook for 1 minute more. Toss in a bowl with the spinach, courgettes, rice and cheese.

3 Heat oven to 200C/180C fan/gas 6 and put in a baking sheet. Cut the pastry in half and roll each piece out on a floured surface to 32 x 17cm. Place one half in a 30 x 15cm tin and prick the base. Beat the large eggs with the mustard and some seasoning. Mix with the spinach mixture.

4 Spoon the mixture into the base. Beat together the milk and medium egg, then use some to brush the edges of the pastry. Lay the other sheet of pastry on top and press down gently to seal. Brush with more egg and sprinkle with the seeds.

5 Place the tin on the hot baking tray and bake for 10 minutes. Reduce oven to 160C/140C fan/gas 3 and bake for a further 30 minutes until golden. Cool.

PER SERVING 631 kcals, protein 18g, carbs 55g, fat 38g, sat fat 13g, fibre 6g, sugar 5g, salt 1.9g

Crispy squashed baby roasties

Try roasting your new potatoes instead of boiling them to really bring out their sweet flavour. Squashing them first gives lots of lovely crispy bits.

TAKES 1 HOUR • SERVES 6

1kg/2lb 4oz small salad or new
    potatoes
4 tbsp olive oil
2 tsp fennel seeds
1 tbsp flaky sea salt

1 Boil the potatoes for 10 minutes until tender, then drain and leave to steam-dry. Heat oven to 200C/180C fan/gas 6.
2 Drizzle half the oil over a flat, sturdy baking tray and tip in the potatoes. Add the fennel seeds, and season with the flaky sea salt and some black pepper, tossing everything to coat. Gently squash the potatoes with a potato masher to just break the skins. Drizzle with the remaining oil and bake for 45 minutes until crispy and golden.

PER SERVING 183 kcals, protein 3g, carbs 25g, fat 8g, sat fat 1g, fibre 2g, sugar 2g, salt 1.7g

Garlicky green beans

A delicious new way to serve green beans – try them as a side with Squash & blue-cheese Wellington on page 80.

TAKES 10 MINUTES ● **SERVES 6**
300g/10oz green beans, trimmed
2 garlic cloves, sliced
2 tbsp olive oil

1 Cook the green beans in boiling water for 2–3 minutes until just tender, then drain well and steam-dry for a minute.
2 Meanwhile, gently fry the garlic in the oil until pale golden – no longer. Toss with the beans, season and serve.

PER SERVING 50 kcals, protein 1g, carbs 2g, fat 4g, sat fat 1g, fibre 2g, sugar 2g, salt none

Braised leeks & peas

A lovely springtime accompaniment to your Sunday lunch. Use fresh peas when they are in season – they will be supersweet.

TAKES 25 MINUTES ● **SERVES 6**

6 leeks, trimmed
250ml/9fl oz chicken or vegetable stock
3 garlic cloves, sliced
4 thyme sprigs, plus extra leaves
    to garnish
200g/7oz fresh or frozen peas
2 tsp olive oil

1 Discard the outer, darker, tougher leaves from the leeks, then halve each into two shorter lengths and rinse under cold running water.

2 Pour the chicken or veg stock into a large, wide shallow pan, then scatter in the garlic and thyme sprigs. Lay the leeks in the pan, trying not to crowd them, then season with black pepper. Cover and simmer for 15 minutes until almost tender. Tip in the peas, bring back to the boil and simmer for a further 5 minutes until the veg is cooked. Using a slotted spoon, transfer the leeks, peas and garlic to a warm serving dish, season with extra pepper, drizzle over the olive oil and finish with a scattering of thyme leaves.

PER SERVING 56 kcals, protein 3.6g, carbs 6.1g, fat 1.9g, sat fat 0.3g, fibre 3.5g, sugar 2.5g, salt 0.4g

Minty carrot, pistachio & feta salad

A vegetarian side salad with cumin-roasted carrots and chickpeas, combined with fresh mint, nuts, spinach and salty cheese – great with Moroccan food.

TAKES 50 MINUTES • SERVES 6

2 tbsp olive oil, plus a little extra for drizzling

500g/1lb 2oz carrots, halved and cut into chunks

400g can chickpeas, drained and rinsed

2 tsp ground cumin

juice ½ lemon

1 tbsp clear honey

small bunch mint, chopped

2 big handfuls spinach leaves

100g bag shelled pistachio nuts, roughly chopped

200g pack feta, crumbled

1 Heat oven to 200C/180C fan/gas 6. Tip 1 tablespoon of the oil, the carrots, chickpeas and cumin on to a baking tray, season and toss to coat. Roast for 30 minutes or until the carrots are tender.

2 Mix together the lemon juice, honey and remaining oil, then pour all over the roasted carrots and chickpeas. Leave to cool. You can chill the salad at this stage, for up to 1 day; just bring it out of the fridge 1 hour before serving.

3 Mix through the mint, spinach leaves and pistachios to serve, and check the seasoning. Scatter over the feta and drizzle with a little extra oil.

PER SERVING 307 kcals, protein 12g, carbs 20g, fat 20g, sat fat 6g, fibre 6g, sugar 10g, salt 1.6g

Cheesy-chard gratin

Double cream turns green and flavoursome chard into something superindulgent – be sure to mop up all the Gruyère sauce with some warm crusty bread.

TAKES 50 MINUTES • SERVES 4

1 bunch chard (about 350g/12oz)
150ml/¼ pint double cream
1 tbsp wholegrain mustard
140g/5oz Gruyère, coarsely grated
butter, for greasing
2 tbsp finely grated Parmesan (or vegetarian alternative)

1 Heat oven to 200C/180C fan/gas 6. Strip the chard leaves from the stalks, then cut the stalks into sticks. Bring a pan of water to the boil and cook the stalks for 3–4 minutes until starting to soften. Then throw in the leaves for a few moments too so that they just wilt. Drain well.

2 Mix the cream with the mustard, then toss through the chard with most of the Gruyère. Grease a medium gratin dish, spread the chard mix over, then scatter with the remaining Gruyère and the Parmesan. Bake for 30 minutes until bubbling and golden. Serve straight from the dish.

PER SERVING 391 kcals, protein 15g, carbs 3g, fat 36g, sat fat 22g, fibre none, sugar 1g, salt 1.4g

Spiced roast side of salmon

Swap a joint of meat for a side of salmon for something different on a Sunday. This one is spiced up with ginger, paprika and mustard.

TAKES 30 MINUTES • SERVES 6

1.5kg/3lb side of salmon, skin on
1 tbsp olive oil, plus extra for brushing
½ tsp ground ginger
1 tsp paprika
½ tsp coarsely ground black peppercorns
1 tbsp wholegrain mustard
1 tsp honey
1 lemon, cut into wedges, to garnish

1 Heat oven to 200C/180C fan/gas 6. Line a big roasting tin with baking parchment or foil – this helps to prevent the fish from sticking to the tin as it cooks. Brush the salmon skin with the extra oil and place it, skin-side down, on the paper or foil.
2 Mix the ground ginger with the paprika, pepper, mustard, honey. Spread it evenly over the fleshy side of the fish.
3 Roast, uncovered, for about 20 minutes until the salmon is cooked through – check by poking a knife into the fillet and making sure the fish flakes easily.
4 Serve directly from the tin, or use a couple of fish slices to carefully lift the salmon on to a big plate. Slice into portions and serve with lemon wedges on the side.

PER SERVING 482 kcals, protein 51g, carbs 2g, fat 30g, sat fat 5g, fibre none, sugar 1g, salt 0.4g

Sticky citrus chicken with carrots & cashews

This easy one-pan dish makes a refreshing change from simple roast chicken. Serve with basmati rice.

TAKES 1¼ HOURS • SERVES 4

8 chicken thighs
300–400g/11–14oz baby carrots
2 onions, cut into thick round slices
1 tbsp sunflower oil
50g/2oz roasted cashews
small pack coriander, to garnish
boiled basmati rice, to serve

FOR THE GLAZE

100g/4oz clear honey
4 tbsp hot chilli sauce
zest 1 lime, plus 4 tbsp juice (about 2 limes)
zest ½ orange, plus 2 tbsp juice
1 tbsp rice vinegar
1 tbsp tomato purée
2 balls stem ginger, finely chopped, plus 1 tbsp syrup

1 Heat oven to 200C/180C fan/gas 6. Toss the chicken thighs, carrots, onions and oil in a big shallow roasting tin with some seasoning. Roast for 30 minutes.

2 Meanwhile, whisk together the glaze ingredients. Drizzle all over the chicken and veg, then roast for a further 15 minutes.

3 Scatter over the cashews, mix everything together well, then roast for a further 15 minutes until the chicken is browned, tender and sticky. Scatter over some coriander leaves and serve with boiled basmati rice.

PER SERVING 550 kcals, protein 31g, carbs 39g, fat 30g, sat fat 7g, fibre 6g, sugar 36g, salt 1.4g

Pulled lamb shoulder with pomegranate glaze

Tender enough to shred and pile into warm pitta bread, or serve with salad.

TAKES 5 HOURS 20 MINUTES, PLUS MARINATING • SERVES 6

1.5kg/3lb bone-in lamb shoulder joint
2 red onions, cut into wedges
1 litre carton pomegranate juice
2 tbsp clear honey
100g tub pomegranate seeds, or seeds
   from 1 fresh pomegranate
250g/9oz natural yogurt
small handful mint leaves, chopped

FOR THE MARINADE

4 garlic cloves, chopped
2 tsp each ground cinnamon and cumin
1 tbsp dried oregano
1 lemon, quartered, pips removed
1 teaspoon salt
2 teaspoons black pepper

1 Blend the marinade ingredients in a blender until smooth. Put the lamb in a large foil-lined roasting tin and tip the marinade over the top. Massage all over and leave for 24 hours in the fridge.

2 Take the lamb from the fridge 1 hour before cooking. Heat oven to 160C/140C fan/gas 3. Scatter the onions under and around the lamb, then pour over the pomegranate juice. Cover the lamb with foil and cook for 4 hours.

3 Remove the foil and pour the juices from the tin into a pan with the honey. Increase oven to 220C/200C fan/gas 7, cover the lamb and cook for 30 minutes. Meanwhile, bubble the cooking liquid over a high heat until reduced and syrupy.

4 Pour the glaze over the lamb and cook for another 30 minutes, uncovered, until the glaze starts to char and the lamb is tender. Mix most of the pomegranate seeds, the yogurt and mint leaves in a small bowl. Scatter the remaining seeds over the lamb and serve with the sticky onions and the minty yogurt.

PER SERVING 668 kcals, protein 46g, carbs 33g, fat 39g, sat fat 19g, fibre 1g, sugar 32g, salt 1.3g

Tandoori-roast chicken

Spice up roast chicken with a tandoori-style marinade. The longer you leave it to absorb all the flavours in the fridge, the tastier it will be!

TAKES 2 HOURS, PLUS MARINATING

● **SERVES 4–6**

1.8kg/4lb chicken

2 onions, thickly sliced

1 lemon, halved

thumb-size piece ginger, peeled and thickly sliced

400ml can coconut milk

small bunch coriander, roughly chopped

FOR THE MARINADE

150g pot natural yogurt

1 tbsp tomato purée

juice 1 lemon

1 tsp each hot chilli powder, turmeric, ground coriander, ground cumin, garam masala and ground cinnamon

6 garlic cloves and ½ finger-length piece ginger, whizzed to a paste together

few drops red food colouring (optional)

1 Mix the marinade ingredients with 2 teaspoons salt and 1 teaspoon black pepper. Slash the legs of the chicken a few times, then rub the marinade all over. Marinate in the fridge for at least 2 hours.

2 Heat oven to 200C/180C fan/gas 6. Put the onions, lemon halves and ginger in a roasting tin. Sit the chicken on top and roast for 1½ hours or until the thigh juices run clear when tested with a skewer.

3 When the chicken is done, lift out of the tin, into a dish, cover loosely with foil and leave to rest. Fish out the ginger from the tin and discard. Scrape out the roasted middles from the lemons into a food processor, add the onions and any pan juices, and whizz to a purée. Scrape the purée back into the tin and sit on the hob. Stir in the coconut milk and bubble gently, scraping up any chicken bits from the base of the tin. Add a splash of water if the sauce is too thick. Stir in the coriander and serve with the chicken.

PER SERVING(6) 482 kcals, protein 43g, carbs 12g, fat 30g, sat fat 8g, fibre 1g, sugar 9g, salt 0.7g

Spiced braised-beef pie

This tender, slow-cooked beef pie is richly flavoured and seriously sumptuous.

TAKES 2 HOURS 20 MINUTES

● **SERVES 6**

2 tbsp vegetable oil

1kg/2lb 4oz good-quality braising
    steaks, cut into 2.5cm/1in chunks

1 large onion, finely chopped

2 garlic cloves, finely chopped

small piece ginger, finely chopped

2 tsp Sichuan peppercorns, crushed

25g/1oz plain flour, plus a little extra
    for dusting

1 tbsp tomato purée

3 medium carrots, cut into large
    chunks

2 star anise

1 cinnamon stick

100ml/3½fl oz soy sauce

3 red chillies, left whole but pierced

375g pack ready rolled all-butter
    puff pastry

1 egg, beaten

1 Heat half the oil in a heavy-based flameproof casserole on a medium heat. Fry the meat in batches until browned, then remove from the pan and set aside.

2 Turn down the heat, add the remaining oil to the pan and cook the onion, garlic and ginger for a few minutes. Add the peppercorns to the flour and mix well, then add to the pan to coat the onion. Return the meat to the pan along with the tomato purée, carrots, star anise and cinnamon. Stir then cook for 1 minute.

3 Add the soy sauce, chillies and 450ml/¾ pint water, and simmer for 1½ hours until the meat is tender. Leave to cool.

4 Heat oven to 190C/170C fan/gas 5. Once cool, spoon the filling into a 2-litre pie dish, removing the cinnamon, chillies and star anise. Roll out the pastry on a floured surface until 2cm/¾in larger than the dish. Put a pie funnel in the middle of the pie. Brush the edges of the dish with some egg, then lay the pastry over the top and press down well. Pierce the centre and trim off excess pastry with a knife. Brush with egg and bake for 30–35 minutes.

PER SERVING 586 kcals, protein 40g, carbs 34g, fat 32g, sat fat 13g, fibre 3g, sugar 9g, salt 5.6g

Chicken mole

This Mexican chicken stew is flavoured with chilli and enriched with dark chocolate.

TAKES 2½ HOURS ● SERVES 6

2 dried ancho chillies
8 bone-in chicken thighs, skin removed
2 tbsp sunflower oil
2 onions, chopped
2 tsp ground cumin
1½ tsp ground cinnamon
3 garlic cloves, roughly chopped
50g/2oz raisins
2 tbsp chipotle paste
2 tbsp smooth peanut butter
400g can chopped tomatoes
25g/1oz dark chocolate (look for one
    with at least 70% cocoa solids)
1 small red onion, sliced into rings
juice 1 lime
cooked basmati rice and soured cream,
    to serve (optional)

1 Soak the chillies in boiling water for 20 minutes. Season the chicken. Heat the oil in a flameproof casserole dish, and brown the chicken all over. Remove to a plate. Add the onions to the pan and cook for 5 minutes. Add the spices and cook for 1 minute.

2 Remove the chillies, reserving the liquid, and discard the stalks and seeds. Whizz to a paste in a blender with 4 tablespoons of the soaking liquid, the garlic and raisins. Tip into the pan. Add the chipotle, peanut butter, tomatoes and 400ml/14fl oz water. Return the chicken to the pan and season. Cover and simmer, stirring occasionally, for 1 hour.

3 Remove the chicken pieces to a plate. Shred the meat and discard the bones. Return the shredded chicken to the sauce, add the chocolate and cook, uncovered, for 30 minutes. Add water, if it gets too thick.

4 Meanwhile, put the red onion in a small bowl. Add the lime juice and a pinch of salt. Leave to pickle until ready to serve.

5 Remove the mole from the heat, scatter with the pickled red onion and serve with rice and soured cream, if you like.

PER SERVING 690 kcals, protein 28g, carbs 93g, fat 22g, sat fat 5g, fibre 3g, sugar 13g, salt 0.5g

Spiced roast lamb

This lighter, spiced-up version of roast lamb is perfect for a summer supper in the garden. Serve with a simple tomato and lentil salad and spicy poppadums.

TAKES 2 HOURS, PLUS MARINATING
● **SERVES 4–6**

2kg/4lb 8oz leg of lamb

FOR THE MARINADE

140g/5oz natural full-fat yogurt
1 thumb-size piece ginger, finely grated
3 large garlic cloves, crushed
1 tbsp tomato purée
juice ½ lime
1 tsp each ground cumin, turmeric
  powder, crushed chilli flakes and
  fennel seeds, lightly crushed
handful coriander leaves, finely
  chopped

1 Stir together the marinade ingredients and season with ½ teaspoon ground black pepper and 1½ teaspoons flaky salt. Slash the lamb several times on both sides, then massage the marinade all over it. Seal into a large food bag or non-metallic container and chill overnight (or at least for a few hours). Let the lamb sit at room temperature for 2 hours before roasting.
2 Heat oven to 220C/200C fan/gas 7. Put the lamb into a foil-lined roasting tin and roast for 20 minutes. Turn the oven down to 190C/170C fan/gas 5 and roast for 1 hour 20 minutes for meat that's pink near the bone. Cover loosely with foil halfway through cooking or once the marinade has charred and the meat looks golden. Leave the lamb to rest for 20 minutes before carving.

PER SERVING (6) 417 kcals, protein 48g, carbs 3g, fat 24g, sat fat 10g, fibre none, sugar 2g, salt 0.8g

Shredded sesame-chicken pancakes with spiced plum sauce

Love crispy roast duck? Then you'll love digging in to this tasty variation.

TAKES 2 HOURS 35 MINUTES

● **SERVES 4–6**

1.8kg/4lb whole chicken

2 tbsp sunflower oil

2 tbsp five spice powder

2 tbsp clear honey

2 tbsp sesame seeds

FOR THE PLUM SAUCE

6 plums, stones removed and
    quartered

3 tbsp soft brown sugar

2 tsp five spice powder

1 tsp cornflour

100ml/3½fl oz rice wine vinegar or
    sherry

TO SERVE

soft Chinese pancakes or wraps,
    warmed

½ cucumber, finely shredded

6 spring onions, finely shredded

1 Heat oven to 200C/180C fan/gas 6. Sit the chicken in a roasting tin, drizzle with oil and rub all over with the five spice and season well. Roast for 30 minutes.

2 Turn the oven down to 160C/140C fan/gas 3 and cook for 1 hour 50 minutes.

3 Prepare the sauce. Toss everything except the vinegar together in a separate roasting tin, then pour in the vinegar, mix again and set aside.

4 Remove the chicken from the oven; increase oven to 200C/180C fan/gas 6. Drizzle over the honey and sprinkle with seeds. Return to the oven for 20 minutes, with the plums on the shelf underneath. When the chicken is cooked, remove from the oven. Leave to rest covered with foil for 20 minutes. Cook the plums for 15 minutes more, until they are soft and the sauce is thick.

5 To serve, shred the chicken and pile into pancakes with the warm plum sauce, the cucumber and the spring onions.

PER SERVING (6) 433 kcals, protein 38g,
carbs 19g, fat 23g, sat fat 6g, fibre 2g, sugar 19g,
salt 0.5g

Ginger & sesame sprouts

Give sprouts an Asian twist with ginger and toasted sesame seeds.

TAKES 15 MINUTES ● SERVES 8

800g/1lb 12oz Brussels sprouts,
   trimmed and halved
1 tbsp sesame oil
small piece ginger, peeled and
   shredded
4 tbsp toasted sesame seeds

1 Blanch the sprouts in boiling water for 3 minutes, then drain well.
2 Heat most of the oil in a wok and add the ginger. Sizzle for a moment, then add the sprouts and stir-fry until hot. Scatter over the sesame seeds and drizzle with a touch more oil. Season with salt, if you like, and serve.

PER SERVING 100 kcals, protein 5g, carbs 4g, fat 7g, sat fat 1g, fibre 5g, sugar 3g, salt none

Chipotle hasselback sweet potatoes

A new way to serve healthy sweet potatoes; the perfect accompaniment to a chilli con carne.

TAKES 1 HOUR 10 MINUTES
- **SERVES 4**

4 sweet potatoes
2 tbsp olive oil
1 tbsp chipotle paste
zest and juice 1 lime
handful coriander leaves, to scatter

1 Heat oven to 200C/180C fan/gas 6. Slice the potatoes about three-quarters of the way through at 1cm/½in intervals. Brush with ½ tablespoon of the olive oil, place on a baking tray and bake for 35–40 minutes. Meanwhile, mix together the remaining oil, the chipotle, lime zest and juice.

2 Remove the potatoes from the oven and brush all over, and down into the slits, with the chipotle mixture. Return to the oven for another 15–20 minutes or until cooked through. Scatter with the coriander leaves just before serving.

PER SERVING 226 kcals, protein 3g, carbs 40g, fat 6g, sat fat 1g, fibre 5g, sugar 11g, salt 0.3g

Honey-roasted swede with chilli & cumin

Swede is an underused vegetable, but it's cheap, tasty and healthy, and is transformed into a delicious side dish in this recipe.

TAKES 1 HOUR • SERVES 4

1 large swede, peeled and cut into large chunks
2 tbsp olive oil
1 tbsp clear honey
1 tsp cumin seeds
1 large red chilli, deseeded and chopped
small bunch coriander, chopped

1 Heat oven to 200C/180C fan/gas 6. Toss the swede in the olive oil in a shallow roasting tin, then season. Roast in the oven for 35–40 minutes, tossing occasionally, until the swede is golden and soft.

2 Stir in the honey and cumin seeds, and continue to roast for 10 minutes until just starting to catch. Remove and stir through the chilli and coriander to serve.

PER SERVING 97 kcals, protein 1g, carbs 10g, fat 6g, sat 1g, fibre 3g, sugar 10g, salt 0.1g

Spring cabbage with mustard seeds

Stir-frying cabbage not only retains many of the vitamins that would be lost in boiling but also enhances its delicious flavour.

TAKES 15 MINUTES • SERVES 4

1 tbsp olive oil
1 tbsp mustard seeds
1 small onion, finely sliced
1 garlic clove, crushed
1 tbsp grated ginger
500g/1lb 2oz spring cabbage, shredded

1 Heat the oil in a frying pan, then cook the mustard seeds until they are fragrant and starting to pop. Add the onion, garlic and ginger, then fry until golden. Tip in the cabbage and stir to coat in the spices, then cook for 5 minutes until tender. Season and serve immediately.

PER SERVING 65 kcals, protein 3g, carbs 6g, fat 4g, sat fat 1g, fibre 3g, sugar 6g, salt none

Mustard-glazed roasted new potatoes

New potatoes are at their most flavoursome in the spring, with Jersey Royals being the top of the crop.

TAKES 1 HOUR • SERVES 8

1.25kg/2lb 12oz new potatoes, halved
3 thyme sprigs
3 tbsp extra-virgin olive oil
1 tbsp wholegrain mustard

1 Heat oven to 230C/210C fan/gas 8. Arrange the potatoes on a large baking tray. Add the thyme, drizzle with 2 tablespoons of the olive oil, season and toss to coat. Cook in the oven for 50 minutes or until crisp.
2 To finish the potatoes, toss with the mustard, drizzle with the remaining olive oil, season and serve.

PER SERVING 149 kcals, protein 3g, carbs 24g, fat 5g, sat fat 1g, fibre 2g, sugar 2g, salt 0.1g

Stir-fried broccoli with coconut

Fresh curry leaves will really enhance the flavour of this side dish. They are now sold in some supermarkets, but if you can't find them, dried will work too.

TAKES 20 MINUTES • SERVES 10

6 tbsp vegetable oil
3½ tsp mustard seeds
3 tbsp fresh or dried curry leaves
pinch chilli flakes
4 red onions, thickly sliced
100g/4oz ginger, shredded
800g/1lb 12oz thin-stemmed broccoli, cut into bite-size pieces
100g/4oz fresh or frozen grated coconut or 3 tbsp desiccated
juice 2 limes

1 Heat the oil in a large wok or pan set over a medium heat. Toss in the mustard seeds followed by the curry leaves (if you are using dried curry leaves, add them later on with the broccoli) and chilli flakes. Swirl everything around until the leaves stop spluttering, then add the onions and ginger, and fry for 3–4 minutes over a high heat.

2 Stir in the broccoli (and dried curry leaves, if using) and continue frying over a high heat until just tender, stirring all the time. Scatter over the coconut (if you are using desiccated coconut, soak it in hot water for 5 minutes before tipping into a sieve, draining away any liquid, and adding to the pan at the end of cooking), stir to mix and sharpen with the lime juice.

PER SERVING 151 kcals, protein 5g, carbs 7g, fat 12g, sat fat 4g, fibre 4g, sugar 5g, salt none

Spinach with chilli & lemon crumbs

Top wilted spinach with lemony breadcrumbs for an extra layer of texture and flavour.

TAKES 10 MINUTES • SERVES 4

25g/1oz butter
100g/4oz fresh breadcrumbs
zest 1 lemon
2 garlic cloves, crushed
1 red chilli, finely chopped
500g/1lb 2oz spinach leaves

1 Melt the butter in a large frying pan and then, when it starts to foam, tip in the breadcrumbs, zest, garlic and chilli. Cook until golden and crunchy. Remove from the pan, season and set aside.
2 Add the spinach to the pan and wilt, stirring. Season and serve with the crunchy crumbs sprinkled over the top.

PER SERVING 169 kcals, protein 7g, carbs 20g, fat 7g, sat fat 3g, fibre 3g, sugar 3g, salt 1g

Turkey, Brie & cranberry Wellington

Turkey breasts are easy to find year round and are cheaper to use than a whole bird.

TAKES 2 HOURS 5 MINUTES

● **SERVES 8**

FOR THE FILLING

2 turkey breasts
200g/7oz Brie, sliced
4–5 tbsp cranberry sauce

FOR THE STUFFING

2 tbsp butter
1 leek, finely sliced
100g/4oz gammon, chopped
5 sage leaves, chopped
4 sausages, skins removed
85g/3oz fresh breadcrumbs

FOR THE PASTRY

2 x 500g blocks all-butter puff pastry
plain flour, for dusting
1 egg, beaten

1 Trim the turkey breasts to create a long tube of meat, saving any trimmings. Slice a deep pocket into each breast and divide the cranberry sauce and Brie between them. Chill while you make the stuffing.

2 Melt the butter in a pan and add the leek for about 5 minutes. Finely chop the turkey trimmings and add to the pan with the gammon. Cook for 5 minutes, then allow to cool slightly. Mix with the sage, sausage meat and breadcrumbs. Season.

3 Roll out 1 pastry block on a floured surface to 5cm/2in larger than the turkey breasts. Lift on to a baking sheet; top with the turkey, then the stuffing. Roll out the remaining pastry, brush the edge of the bottom sheet with egg and lay over the top one. Trim the edges then crimp together.

4 Heat oven to 200C/180C fan/gas 6. Brush the Wellington with egg and score a criss-cross pattern. Cook for 30 minutes, then cover with foil and cook for 30–45 minutes more. Check the middle is hot by inserting a skewer for 5 seconds – it should feel hot to the touch. Rest for 15 minutes, then slice to serve.

PER SERVING 783 kcals, protein 28g, carbs 58g, fat 49g, sat fat 24g, fibre 1g, sugar 6g, salt 2.5g

Lamb shank, pea & mint pie

This recipe, perfect for a spring lunch, makes the most of lamb shanks which are much cheaper than a whole leg. Looks special with leaves made from pastry trimmings.

TAKES 4½ HOURS • SERVES 6

2 tbsp sunflower or rapeseed oil
4 lamb shanks
2 onions, chopped
2 rosemary sprigs, leaves finely
   chopped
2 thyme sprigs
300ml/½ pint white wine
1.5 litres/2½ pints good-quality
   chicken stock
25g/1oz butter
3 tbsp plain flour
250g/9oz frozen peas
5 spring onions, finely chopped
small bunch parsley, finely chopped
small bunch mint, finely chopped
1 egg, beaten
325g sheet ready-rolled puff or
   shortcrust pastry

1 Heat oil in a large pan, brown the lamb, then transfer to a plate. Soften the onions and add the rosemary, thyme and wine. Bring to a simmer, then add the stock, lamb and juices. Cover with a tight-fitting lid, reduce the heat and cook for 3 hours – until very tender. Leave until cool.

2 Heat oven to 200C/180C fan/gas 6. Remove the shanks, pull the meat off the bones in big chunks, discarding any fatty bits, put in a pie dish – about 30 x 20cm.

3 Put the stock back on the heat and boil until reduced by half. Meanwhile, in a frying pan, melt the butter, then stir in the flour. Whisk in ladlefuls of the stock until you have a smooth sauce. Taste for seasoning, then tip over the lamb.

4 Add the peas, spring onions and herbs to the lamb; mix to combine. Brush the rim of the dish with some egg. Lift the pastry on to the pie and press down to the edges, crimping to seal. Brush the pie with more egg; bake for 40–45 minutes until golden.

PER SERVING 1081 kcals, protein 62g, carbs 67g, fat 58g, sat fat 28g, fibre 9g, sugar 7g, salt 2.1g

Slow-braised pork shoulder with cider & parsnips

Not only is pork shoulder a cheaper cut of this meat, but it is also full of flavour.

TAKES 2 HOURS 50 MINUTES
- **SERVES 5**

2 tbsp olive oil
1kg/2lb 4oz pork shoulder, diced
2 onions, sliced
2 celery sticks, roughly chopped
3 parsnips, cut into chunks
2 bay leaves
1 tbsp plain flour
330ml bottle cider
850ml/1½ pints chicken stock
handful parsley, chopped, to garnish

1 Heat oven to 180C/160C fan/gas 4. Heat the oil in a large lidded flameproof casserole dish and brown the meat in batches, then set aside. Add the onions, celery and parsnips to the dish with the bay leaves and fry for 10 minutes until golden brown. Sprinkle in the flour and give a good stir, then return the pork and any juices to the dish.

2 Add the cider and stock so that the meat and vegetables are covered. Season and bring to a simmer, then cover and put in the oven for 2 hours. Serve sprinkled with parsley, with mashed potato and greens, if you like.

PER SERVING 534 kcals, protein 46g, carbs 19g, fat 29g, sat fat 9g, fibre 8g, sugar 10g, salt 0.8g

Sausage & stuffing toad-in-the-hole

Make a pack of sausages go further by adding stuffing balls to your toad-in-the-hole.

TAKES 1 HOUR 35 MINUTES
- **SERVES 4**

FOR THE BATTER
140g/5oz plain flour
1 tsp English mustard powder
3 large eggs
300ml/½ pint milk

FOR THE SAUSAGE AND STUFFING
4 tbsp sunflower oil
2 large onions, sliced
85g/3oz pack breadcrumb stuffing mix
small handful sage leaves, chopped
8 sausages

FOR THE GRAVY
2 tbsp plain flour
2 tbsp caramelised onion chutney
2 tsp Marmite
500ml/18fl oz beef stock

1 Whisk together the batter ingredients with a pinch of salt until smooth. Leave to rest for at least 30 minutes.
2 Heat 1 tablespoon of the oil in a small pan. Add the onions with a pinch of salt and cook for 10–15 minutes until soft. Next, make the stuffing according to the pack instructions, adding the sage. Add a quarter of the onions, leaving the rest in the pan. Heat oven to 230C/210C fan/gas 8.
3 Shape the stuffing into eight walnut-size balls. Grease a large roasting dish with the remaining oil. Add the sausages and stuffing balls; cook for 15 minutes.
4 Remove the tin from the oven, loosen the sausages and stuffing from the bottom of the tin, then pour over the rested batter. Return to the oven and bake for 35–40 minutes until puffed and golden.
5 Make the gravy. Add the flour, chutney and Marmite to the onion pan, and mix to a paste. Cook for 2 minutes until bubbling, then slowly stir in the stock. Bubble for 5 minutes. Serve warm with the toad-in-the-hole.

PER SERVING 690 kcals, protein 31g, carbs 54g, fat 39g, sat fat 11g, fibre 4g, sugar 12g, salt 3.3g

Sort-of Scotch broth

A steaming bowl of broth with tender lamb and barley – just the thing to warm you up after a long wintery walk.

TAKES 2¼ HOURS • SERVES 6–8

1 tbsp vegetable oil, plus a bit extra
1kg/2lb 4oz lamb neck fillet, shoulder
    or other fatty stewing lamb, cut into
    generous chunks
1 onion, chopped
2 carrots, roughly chopped
1 leek, chopped
2 celery sticks, chopped
3 thyme sprigs
1 bay leaf
1 small white cabbage, roughly
    shredded
300g/11oz swede, diced the same size
    as the carrot
200g/7oz pot or pearl barley
2 litres/3½ pints vegetable stock
large handful parsley, chopped,
    to garnish

1 Heat oven to 160C/140C fan/gas 3. Heat the oil in a flameproof casserole dish and brown the lamb – in batches if necessary – then remove to a plate with a slotted spoon. Add a drizzle more oil and tip in the onion, carrots, leek, celery, thyme and bay. Cook for 5 minutes until the vegetables start to soften.

2 Stir in the cabbage, swede and barley, then return the meat to the pan. Pour over the stock and season with a little salt and lots of pepper. Bring to a simmer, cover with a lid and cook in the oven for 1½ hours until the meat and barley are tender and the vegetables are just starting to collapse. Scatter with parsley and ladle into bowls.

PER SERVING (8) 452 kcals, protein 27g, carbs 29g, fat 25g, sat fat 11g, fibre 5g, sugar 8g, salt 0.9g

Lighter puffed salmon & spinach fish pie

Frozen fish fillets can be much cheaper than fresh but are still packed with flavour.

TAKES 1¼ HOURS ● SERVES 6

1kg/2lb 4oz Maris Piper potatoes, cut into large chunks

2 large eggs, separated

400g/14oz frozen whole-leaf spinach (frozen weight), defrosted and squeezed dry

85g/3oz reduced-fat mature Cheddar

whole nutmeg, for grating

FOR THE FILLING

500g/1lb 2oz fish, a mix of white and salmon (we used 2 frozen salmon fillets and 2 cod, defrosted)

1 onion, halved

few whole cloves

1 fresh or dried bay leaf

300ml/½ pint semi-skimmed milk

300ml/½ pint fish stock (from a cube is fine)

25g/1oz butter

2 tbsp extra-virgin olive oil

50g/2oz plain flour

1 tsp wholegrain mustard

1 Boil the potatoes for 20 minutes until tender. Meanwhile, put the fish in a frying pan, skin-side down. Stud the onion with the cloves and add to the pan with the bay, milk and stock. Bring to the boil, then cover and simmer for 2 minutes. Remove the cod, then cover and cook the salmon for another 3 minutes. Set the fish aside. Strain and reserve the cooking liquid.

2 In another pan, melt the butter with the oil, stir in the flour and cook for 2 minutes until it smells toasty. Take off the heat and slowly whisk in the cooking liquid. Return to the heat, whisk until the sauce boils and thickens, then stir in the mustard.

3 Heat oven to 180C/160C fan/gas 4. Drain and mash the potatoes, then beat in the egg yolks, spinach and most of the cheese. Season and add nutmeg. Whisk the egg whites to soft peaks, then fold into the potato in two batches.

4 Flake the fish into a large ovenproof dish, add the sauce and top with the potato mix. Scatter with the remaining cheese and bake for 35–40 minutes until golden.

PER SERVING 449 kcals, protein 33g, carbs 37g, fat 18g, sat fat 6g, fibre 6g, sugar 5g, salt 0.8g

Pot-roast beef with French-onion gravy

These cheaper, leaner cuts of meat are well-suited to slow-cooking.

TAKES 2½ HOURS • SERVES 4

1kg/2lb 4oz silverside or topside of
   beef, trimmed of fat

2 tbsp olive oil

8 young carrots, tops trimmed (but
   leave a little stalk, if you like)

1 celery stick, finely chopped

200ml/7fl oz white wine

600ml/1 pint rich beef stock

2 bay leaves

500g/1lb 2oz onions, thinly sliced

a few thyme sprigs

1 tsp butter

1 tsp light soft brown or light
   muscovado sugar

2 tsp plain flour

1 Heat oven to 160C/140C fan/gas 3. Rub the meat with 1 teaspoon of the oil and season. Heat a flameproof casserole and brown the meat for 10 minutes. Meanwhile, add 2 teaspoons of the oil to a pan and fry the carrots and celery for 10 minutes.

2 Lift the beef on to a plate, splash the wine into the hot casserole and boil for 2 minutes. Pour in the stock, return the beef, then tuck in the carrots, celery and bay leaves. Cover and cook in the oven for 2 hours, turning the beef after 1 hour.

3 Heat the remaining oil in a pan and stir in the onions and thyme. Season. Cover and cook gently for 20 minutes until soft. Remove the lid, turn up the heat, add the butter and sugar, then caramelise the onions to a dark golden brown, stirring often. Remove the thyme. Set aside.

4 When the beef is tender, remove from the casserole and cut the strings. Reheat the onions, stir in the flour and cook for 1 minute. Whisk in the meat juices to make a thick gravy. Put the beef and carrots back in the casserole to serve.

PER SERVING 487 kcals, protein 6g, carbs 19g, fat 17g, sat fat 5g, fibre 5g, sugar 15g, salt 1g

Chard-stuffed roast lamb

Shoulder of lamb is even more delicious when stuffed with Mediterranean flavour.

TAKES 1¾ HOURS • SERVES 6

large bunch chard (about 500g/1lb 2oz
 – rainbow chard looks pretty), leaves
 and stalks separated
4 tbsp olive oil
25g/1oz pine nuts
large handful raisins
2 handfuls pitted large green olives,
 chopped
200ml/7fl oz white wine
1 boned shoulder of lamb (about
 1.5kg/3lb boned weight), rolled and
 loosely tied

1 Heat oven to 220C/200C fan/gas 7. Shred the chard leaves, cut the stalks into batons and set the stalks aside. Heat half the oil in a frying pan, add the leaves and cook for 2 minutes until completely wilted, then tip into a bowl. Add the pine nuts, raisins and olives, a tiny drizzle of olive oil, a small splash of the wine and some seasoning. Mix well.

2 Place the lamb on a board and push as much of the stuffing as you can into the cavity along the meat. Don't worry if any of the stuffing falls out, but make sure you keep it. Scatter the chard stalks over the bottom of a shallow roasting tin and add any stray stuffing. Nestle the lamb among the stalks and pour the remaining wine over everything. Rub the lamb with the remaining olive oil, season with sea salt and ground black pepper, and put in the oven for 1 hour.

3 Remove the meat from the oven and leave to rest for 15 minutes, then serve in thick slices with the braised stalks.

PER SERVING 543 kcals, protein 38g, carbs 6g, fat 39g, sat fat 14g, fibre none, sugar 4g, salt 1g

Creamy leek, potato & ham pie

Fill shortcrust pastry with sweet leeks, cheese, cooked ham and a chive and crème fraîche sauce for a Sunday lunch with a difference.

TAKES 1¾ HOURS ● SERVES 6–8

500g pack shortcrust pastry

FOR THE FILLING

2 tbsp olive oil

1 onion, finely chopped

500g/1lb 2oz leeks, cleaned and roughly chopped

3 garlic cloves, finely chopped

3 tbsp snipped chives

600g/1lb 6oz small floury potatoes, roughly the same size, boiled for 5 mins, then drained and cooled

150ml/¼ pint half-fat crème fraîche

200g/7oz Cheddar or Lancashire cheese, grated

200g/7oz thinly sliced ham

1 medium egg, beaten

1 Heat the oil in a pan. Add the onion and leeks, cook for 15 minutes until tender. Add the garlic, cook for 1 minute, then tip into a bowl. Cool. Stir in the chives.

2 Heat oven to 180C/160C fan/gas 4. Put a baking tray in the oven. Roll out half the pastry on a floured surface to 5mm/¼in thick. Use to line a 24cm-round pie tin. Prick the pastry with a fork, put on the baking tray and bake for 10–12 minutes. Return the baking tray to the oven.

3 Slice the cooked potatoes into thin rounds. Mix with the leek mixture, the crème fraiche, cheese and ham, then layer into the pie dish.

4 Roll out remaining pastry to about a 26cm/10in circle. Brush the edge of the base pastry with egg. Lay the circle of pastry over the top and trim the edges, crimping to seal. Brush with the egg. Place on the baking tray and bake for 45 minutes until golden. Cool, then serve.

PER SERVING (8) 511 kcals, protein 19g, carbs 43g, fat 29g, sat fat 16g, fibre 4g, sugar 4g, salt 1.4g

Sausage & veg one-pot

This summery version of a sausage casserole is full of flavour but much lighter than the classic. Serve with bread or mashed potato.

TAKES 1 HOUR 5 MINUTES • SERVES 4

1 tbsp olive oil
12 good-quality sausages
1 small onion, chopped
1 fennel bulb, quartered, then sliced
2 garlic cloves, crushed
½ red chilli, finely chopped
2 tsp fennel seeds
2 tbsp plain flour
150ml/¼ pint white wine
500ml/18fl oz chicken stock
200g pack green beans, halved
300g/11oz broad beans, double podded
    (unpodded weight)
300g/11oz peas
200g pot half-fat crème fraîche
zest 1 lemon, juice ½
handful each parsley and basil leaves,
    chopped
½ red chilli, finely chopped, to garnish
bread or mash, to serve

1 Heat the oil in a large pan. Add the sausages, cook for a few minutes until browned all over, then remove. Tip the onion and fennel into the pan and cook for 10–15 minutes until soft, then add the garlic, half the chilli and the fennel seeds. Cook for a few minutes more, moving everything around the pan now and then, to prevent the garlic burning.

2 Stir the flour into the vegetables, and cook for 1 minute. Pour in the wine, let it bubble for 1 minute, give everything a good stir, then add the stock and return the sausages to the pan, seasoning well. Cover, then gently simmer for 30 minutes.

3 Add the green beans, broad beans and peas, then cook, uncovered, for 2 minutes more. Stir in the crème fraîche, lemon zest and juice, and herbs. Add more salt and pepper to taste, sprinkle with the chilli, then serve with plenty of bread or mash for soaking up the juices.

PER SERVING 560 kcals, protein 25g, carbs 29g, fat 36g, sat fat 14g, fibre 10g, sugar 8g, salt 2.7g

Honey–mustard parsnip & potato bake

A frugal, creamy bake using potatoes and parsnips.

TAKES 1 HOUR 35 MINUTES

● **SERVES 6**

800g/1lb 12oz potatoes, such as
   Desirée, cut into 2.5cm/1in cubes
800g/1lb 12oz parsnips, cut into
   2.5cm/1in cubes
85g/3oz butter
85g/3oz plain flour
600ml/1 pint milk
2 tbsp wholegrain mustard
2 tbsp clear honey
2 tbsp white wine vinegar
85g/3oz fresh white bread, whizzed
   to crumbs
25g/1oz Parmesan, grated

1 Bring a large pan of salted water to the boil. Tip in the potatoes and parsnips, bring back to the boil and simmer for 5 minutes. Gently drain so they don't rough up too much, then tip into a baking dish.

2 Melt the butter in a big pan, then stir in the flour and cook for 2 minutes. Gradually stir in the milk to a smooth, lump-free sauce. Cook gently, stirring constantly, until the sauce is nicely thickened – about 5 minutes. Stir in the mustard, honey, vinegar and some seasoning. Pour evenly over the potatoes and parsnips. Mix the crumbs and cheese together, then scatter over the top and set aside until ready to bake. You can cover the dish and chill for up to 24 hours before finishing.

3 Cook the bake at 200C/180C fan/gas 6 for 30–40 minutes until the top is crisp and golden and the sauce is hot through.

PER SERVING 502 kcals, protein 13g, carbs 71g, fat 16g, sat fat 9g, fibre 11g, sugar 19g, salt 0.8g

Baked carrot & sweet potato mash

Try something different with sweet potatoes and carrots. This sweet mash with a crispy topping can be made up to a day before serving, then simply reheated.

TAKES 1 HOUR 10 MINUTES

● **SERVES 8**

800g/1lb 12oz sweet potatoes, peeled
and chopped into 2.5cm/1in cubes
500g/1lb 2oz carrots, chopped into
2.5cm/1in cubes
6 tbsp double cream
good grating nutmeg
small pinch ground cinnamon
large handful fresh breadcrumbs
olive oil, for drizzling

1 Put the veg in a large pan, cover with water and bring to the boil. Put a lid on the pan and cook for 15 minutes until tender. Drain, and leave to steam-dry in the colander for a few minutes.

2 Heat oven to 220C/200C fan/gas 7. Once completely dry, return the veg to the pan and mash with the cream, nutmeg, cinnamon and plenty of seasoning. Transfer the mash to an ovenproof gratin dish, sprinkle with the breadcrumbs and drizzle with a little olive oil.

3 Cook in the oven for 35 minutes until the top is golden and crunchy and the mash is piping hot.

PER SERVING 175 kcals, protein 2g, carbs 26g, fat 7g, sat fat 4g, fibre 4g, sugar 10g, salt 0.2g

Crunchy potato squares with herby salt

Make up this herb-flavoured salt to sprinkle over spuds – any leftover salt will keep for 5 days in a sealed jar. For the best flavours, cook underneath your Sunday roast.

TAKES 1 HOUR 35 MINUTES
- **SERVES 8**

1.25kg/2lb 12oz potatoes, cut into
    2.5cm/1in cubes
3 tbsp vegetable, sunflower or
    rapeseed oil
1 tbsp fine polenta

FOR THE HERBY SALT
6 rosemary sprigs
6 thyme sprigs
3 sage leaves
3 tbsp coarse sea salt

1 To make the herby salt, put all the ingredients in a small food processor (or use a pestle and mortar) and grind to a fine salt.

2 Tip the potatoes into a large roasting tin and toss with the oil, polenta, 2 tablespoons of the herby salt and some black pepper.

3 If you are roasting a joint, bake on the shelf below at 200C/180C fan/gas 6 for 30 minutes. When the meat comes out, increase oven to 220C/200C fan/gas 7 and move the potatoes to the top shelf for another 45 minutes, shaking the tin halfway through the cooking time.

PER SERVING 158 kcals, protein 3g, carbs 26g, fat 5g, sat fat none, fibre 3g, sugar 1g, salt 2.3g

Mustardy baked onions

This is a great way to serve onions as a side dish in their own right – the perfect accompaniment to toad-in-the-hole.

TAKES 55 MINUTES • SERVES 4

4 medium red onions
4 small rosemary sprigs
knob butter
1 tbsp balsamic vinegar
2 tbsp grainy mustard
1 tbsp soft brown sugar

1 Heat oven to 180C/160C fan/gas 4. Slice the root off each onion to create a flat bottom, then carefully peel, leaving the onion whole. Cut a deep cross in the top of each, then poke in a sprig of rosemary, dot with butter and place in a roasting tin. Pour a little of the balsamic vinegar over each one and season. Wrap the tin in foil and bake in the oven for 30 minutes. Meanwhile, mix together the mustard and sugar, and set aside.

2 Remove the tin from the oven, take off the foil and spoon a little of the mustard mixture on to each onion. Return to the oven for 15 minutes, uncovered, to caramelise.

PER SERVING 105 kcals, protein 2g, carbs 17g, fat 3g, sat fat 1g, fibre 2g, sugar 14g, salt 0.3g

Creamy baked cauliflower

Flavoured with bay, mace and nutmeg, this is a great Christmassy side dish.

TAKES 1 HOUR 10 MINUTES

● **SERVES 8**

500ml/18fl oz whole milk

2 small onions, 1 quartered, 1 finely
    chopped

1 blade mace

4 bay leaves (fresh, if you have),
    scrunched in your hand

1kg/2lb 4oz cauliflower, broken into
    large florets

85g/3oz butter, plus a knob

85g/3oz plain flour

grating nutmeg

50g/2oz coarse breadcrumbs (dried
    or stale)

1 Put the milk, quartered onion, mace and bay in a pan and simmer. Turn off the heat and infuse for 1 hour, then strain, discarding the onion, mace and bay.

2 Meanwhile, bring a large pan of water to the boil. Tip in the cauliflower and cook for 5 minutes until just tender. Drain and set aside in a colander to steam-dry.

3 Return the pan to the heat, add the knob of butter and the chopped onion. Cook for 10 minutes until soft but not coloured.

4 In a medium-size pan, melt the butter, then stir in the flour to form a paste. Cook for 2 minutes, then gradually stir in the strained milk. Bring to the boil and simmer, stirring often, until thickened and smooth. Stir in the softened onion and season well with salt and nutmeg.

5 Heat oven to 220C/200C fan/gas 7. Tip the cauliflower into an ovenproof dish and pour over the sauce. Scatter the cauliflower with the breadcrumbs, then bake for 30 minutes until the sauce is bubbling and the top is golden and crisp.

PER SERVING 253 kcals, protein 10g, carbs 23g, fat 14g, sat fat 8g, fibre 4g, sugar 8g, salt 0.38g

All-in-one roast bubble & squeak

Serve this alongside a roast chicken, or use up leftovers from a roast and serve simply with a fried egg.

TAKES 50 MINUTES • SERVES 8

1.25kg/2lb 12oz floury potatoes, peeled and cut into 2.5cm/1in chunks
4 tbsp rapeseed oil
200g/7oz smoked lardons or bacon cut into pieces
700g/1lb 8oz Brussels sprouts

1 Heat oven to 220C/200C fan/gas 7. Bring a pan of water to the boil, then tip in the potatoes. Cook for 4–5 minutes, drain well, then return to the pan. Put on the lid and shake a couple times.
2 Set a heavy-bottomed roasting tin on the hob over a medium heat and add the oil. When the oil is really hot, add the potatoes and fry for a few minutes.
3 Add the bacon and sprouts, mix everything together, then put in the oven and bake for 30 minutes until the bacon is crisp and the sprouts are tender.

PER SERVING 265 kcals, protein 10g, carbs 31g, fat 12g, sat fat 7g, fibre 6g, sugar 4g, salt 0.8g

Braised leeks & apples

Sweet leeks and apples make the perfect pairing. Serve with roast pork or sausages.

TAKES 30 MINUTES ● SERVES 4

3 small leeks, outer leaves removed,
    thickly sliced
2 eating apples, cored and cut into
    wedges
3 thyme sprigs
300ml/½ pint vegetable stock
knob butter

1 Arrange the leeks and apple wedges in a single layer in a wide, shallow casserole dish with a lid. Poke the sprigs of thyme in among the leeks and pour over the stock. Season and dot the butter on top.

2 Place over a medium heat, bring to the boil, then cover and gently simmer for 15 minutes or until the apples and leeks are tender.

PER SERVING 60 kcals, protein 2g, carbs 8g, fat 3g, sat fat 1g, fibre 3g, sugar 7g, salt 0.2g

Jam & white chocolate roly-poly

A suet pudding that's baked instead of steamed.

TAKES 1 HOUR 10 MINUTES
● **SERVES 6**

butter, for greasing
300g/11oz self-raising flour, plus extra
    for dusting
85g/3oz caster sugar
140g/5oz suet
150ml/¼ pint milk, plus a dash
8 tbsp raspberry jam
50g/2oz white chocolate, chopped,
    plus about 25g/1oz, melted
425g carton ready-made custard

1 Heat oven to 180C/160C fan/gas 4. Butter a sheet of baking parchment. Mix the flour with the sugar, suet and a good pinch of salt, then bind with the milk, adding a dash more if needed, to make a soft, but not sticky, dough.
2 Roll out the dough on a floured surface to a 20 x 30cm oblong. Spread with the jam and scatter with the chocolate, leaving a border all the way around.
3 Roll up the dough from one short end so you have a sausage shape, then gently pinch the ends to seal in the jam. Carefully lift on to the baking parchment.
4 Fold the paper up over the ends of the roly-poly, then wrap up quite tightly. Secure with staples or bulldog clips all the way along the roll.
5 Bake for 50 minutes until the roll feels firm and looks golden through the paper. Allow to stand for 5 minutes before cutting, as this will stop the jam flowing out. Drizzle with the melted chocolate and serve with a jug of warmed custard.

PER SERVING 824 kcals, protein 10g, carbs 117g, fat 39g, sat fat 19g, fibre 3g, sugar 57g, salt 0.82g

Crunchy custard-baked apples

Baked apples is a classic comfort pud; these ones are baked with custard and a crunchy granola topping.

TAKES 50 MINUTES • SERVES 4–6

500g carton ready-made custard
6 Bramley apples, halved through the middle and core removed
zest and juice 1 orange
1 tsp ground cinnamon
1 tbsp golden caster sugar
6 tbsp crunchy granola with almonds
cream or ice cream, to serve (optional)

1 Heat oven to 180C/160C fan/gas 4. Pour the custard into a large baking dish. Toss the apples in the orange zest and juice, cinnamon and sugar.

2 Arrange the apples, cut-side up, on top of the custard and drizzle with any extra juice from the bowl. Sprinkle over the granola and bake for 30–40 minutes, until the apples are soft and piping hot – cover after 20 minutes if the granola is getting dark. Serve with a drizzle of cream or a scoop of ice cream, if you like.

PER SERVING (6) 171 kcals, protein 3.9g, carbs 28.3g, fat 4.1g, sat fat 1.6g, fibre 2.7g, sugar 24.2g, salt none

Blueberry-swirl cheesecake

This cheesecake is baked in a rectangular tin, making it really easy to slice and serve – but if you only have a deep 23cm-round tin, this will work too.

TAKES 1 HOUR 20 MINUTES, PLUS COOLING & CHILLING • SERVES 14

300g/11oz digestive biscuits, whizzed to crumbs
140g/5oz butter, melted
275g/10oz golden caster sugar
100g/4oz blueberries
1 tsp cornflour, mixed to a paste with 1 tbsp water
3 x 300g packs full-fat soft cheese
4 tbsp plain flour
2 tsp vanilla extract
3 large eggs
200ml pot soured cream

1 Heat oven to 200C/180C fan/gas 6. Line a 20 x 30cm cake tin with baking parchment. Mix the crumbs and butter. Press down firmly into the base of the tin, then bake for 10 minutes. Cool.

2 Meanwhile, bubble 25g/1oz of the sugar, the blueberries and the cornflour paste in a small pan until saucy. Cool.

3 Whisk the soft cheese with an electric whisk until smooth. Whisk in the remaining sugar, the flour, vanilla, eggs and soured cream until smooth.

4 Pour half the cheesecake mixture over the base, then blob half the blueberry sauce on top. Smooth over the remaining cheesecake mix. Drizzle over the remaining blueberry sauce, then use the end of a spoon to ripple. Bake for 10 minutes, then lower oven to 110C/90C fan/gas ¼ and bake for 30 minutes. Cool in the oven for 1 hour with the door closed, then leave for 1 hour more with door ajar. Chill overnight.

PER BAR 606 kcals, protein 6g, carbs 39g, fat 47g, sat fat 28g, fibre none, sugar 24g, salt 1g

Pear & blackberry crostata

A simple pie that is so easy to assemble and makes the most of what's in season.

TAKES 1 HOUR • SERVES 6
500g pack sweet shortcrust pastry
flour, for dusting
4 tbsp blackberry conserve
140g/5oz blackberries
4 ripe pears, peeled, cored and sliced
icing sugar, for dusting

1 Heat oven to 180C/160C/gas 4. Place a baking tray in the oven to heat up. Roll out two-thirds of the pastry on a lightly floured surface to a 5mm/¼in thick disc. Line a 23cm-round pie tin with the pastry, leaving any excess to overhang the tin. Spoon the blackberry conserve on to the pastry base, spreading it out evenly, then top with the blackberries and slices of pear.
2 Roll out the remaining pastry on a lightly floured surface to 5mm thick. Using a fluted ravioli wheel, cut the dough into 12 x 23cm/4½ x 9in strips. Arrange half the strips at 2cm/¾in intervals across the top of the pie. Repeat crossways with the remaining strips. Press the edges to seal and trim any excess.
3 Place on the hot baking tray on the lowest shelf of the oven and bake for 40 minutes until golden. Set aside for 15 minutes to cool in the tin, dusting with icing sugar. Serve in wedges.

PER SERVING 401 kcals, protein 5g, carbs 59g, fat 16g, sat fat 8g, fibre 6g, sugar 30g, salt 0.4g

Baked apple & toffee crumble

Nothing tops a Sunday roast quite like a steaming hot crumble and custard, and this recipe is hard to beat.

TAKES 1 HOUR 20 MINUTES

● **SERVES 6**

FOR THE APPLE LAYER

100g/4oz raisins

100g/4oz pitted soft dates, snipped into small pieces with scissors

85g/3oz light muscovado sugar

3 tbsp dark rum (or use orange juice)

25g/1oz unsalted butter

1 tsp ground mixed spice

zest and juice 1 lemon

4 Bramley apples, about 800g/1lb 12oz, peeled, cored and cut into 1cm/½in rings

FOR THE CRUMBLE

140g/5oz plain flour

100g/4oz unsalted butter

50g/2oz light muscovado sugar

3 tbsp jumbo oats

25g/1oz flaked almonds (or use other nuts if you like)

custard or ice cream, to serve

1 Heat oven to 190C/170C fan/gas 5. Put everything for the apple layer, except the lemon juice and apples, into a bowl and microwave on High for 1½ minutes until the butter has melted and the sugar is syrupy. Toss in the apples and lemon juice, then spoon into a medium baking dish, making sure the dried fruit is evenly distributed.

2 Rub the flour and butter together, first into fine crumbs, then keep going until the mix forms bigger clumps, a bit like a rough biscuit dough. Stir in the sugar, oats and almonds. Scatter the crumble mix over the fruit, then cover with foil and bake for 1 hour, removing the foil for the final 30 minutes, until golden and bubbling. Rest for 10 minutes, then serve with custard or ice cream.

PER SERVING 485 kcals, protein 5g, carbs 67g, fat 20g, sat fat 11g, fibre 5g, sugar 50g, salt 0.1g

Black Forest pudding

A classic summer pudding is made with summer berries. This version uses darker berries, cherries and grapes, giving the soaked bread a luscious colour and flavour.

TAKES 1 HOUR ● SERVES 6–8

sunflower oil, for greasing

300g/11oz blackberries

300g/11oz dark cherries, halved and pitted, quartered if large

200g/7oz small black seedless grapes

140g/5oz golden caster sugar

200g/7oz blackcurrants

200g/7oz blueberries

4 tbsp crème de cassis (or 2 tbsp Ribena)

400g/14oz medium-sliced white bread, crusts removed and cut in half (save 2 whole slices for the top and base)

1 Oil a 1.5-litre pudding basin. Line with a layer of cling film, overhanging at the top. Put the blackberries, cherries, grapes and sugar in a pan with 3 tablespoons water. Cover and cook until syrupy. Add the currants and blueberries, cook for 2 minutes until the fruit is softened, add the cassis or Ribena. Cool.

2 Cut a circle from 1 slice of bread to fit the base of the basin, and cut and reserve a second circle for the top. Press the smaller circle into the basin.

3 Working round the basin, line with the remaining bread, overlapping the edges of the bread slightly and pressing them into place. Patch gaps with scraps.

4 Spoon the fruit into the bread-lined basin, squishing the fruit down to level it, and pour a little juice over the bread at the edges. Save any extra fruit and juice to serve. Press the remaining bread circle on top. Loosely cover with cling film. Place a plate on top with cans to weigh it down. Chill overnight before serving.

PER SERVING 269 kcals, protein 5g, carbs 54g, fat 1g, sat fat 0g, fibre 4g, sugar 35g, salt 0.6g

Sticky date & raisin pudding

This indulgent steamed pudding makes a lovely change from the traditional Christmas pudding. Best served with toffee sauce and ice cream.

TAKES 4 HOURS ● SERVES 8

250g/9oz stoned dates, roughly chopped

100g/4oz raisins

150ml/¼ pint milk

150ml/¼ pint brandy or rum

140g/5oz butter, softened, plus extra for greasing

50g/2oz soft brown sugar

2 large eggs

175g/6oz self-raising flour

1 tsp ground mixed spice

zest 1 orange

toffee sauce and ice cream, to serve

1 Simmer the dates, raisins, milk and brandy or rum in a pan for 5 minutes until the fruit is soft and the liquid has been absorbed – don't worry if it looks a little curdled. Leave to cool. Meanwhile, butter a 1.2-litre pudding basin.

2 Mix the remaining ingredients in a large bowl until combined, then add the fruit mixture and mix again. Scrape into the pudding basin. Cover with buttered baking parchment, then foil to create a lid. Tie with string to secure.

3 Bring a large pan of water – enough to come halfway up the sides of the pudding basin – to a boil. Place a saucer in the base, then add the pudding basin. Cover with a lid and steam for 2½ hours, topping up with boiling water if the level gets low. Check the pudding is cooked by inserting a skewer into the centre. If the skewer has any uncooked mixture on it, return it to the pan to steam for another 15 minutes, then check again.

PER SERVING 418 kcals, protein 6g, carbs 50g, fat 17g, sat fat 10g, fibre 3g, sugar 36g, salt 0.6g

Bakewell-sponge pudding

Sweet cherries topped with a rich almond sponge – heaven in a bowl, just add cream or custard.

TAKES 1 HOUR • SERVES 6

2 x 425g cans pitted black cherries
6 tbsp cherry jam
200g/7oz butter, softened
200g/7oz golden caster sugar
3 large eggs
50g/2oz self-raising flour
140g/4oz ground almonds
1 tsp almond extract
50g/2oz flaked almonds
icing sugar, for dusting
cream or vanilla custard, to serve

1 Heat oven to 180C/160C fan/gas 4. Tip the cherries, and any syrup from the can, and the jam, into a pan. Boil for 10–15 minutes, until the liquid has reduced by half and is thick and syrupy, then pour into a baking dish, roughly 18 x 25cm.

2 In a large bowl, mix the butter, sugar, eggs, flour, almonds, almond extract and a pinch of salt with an electric whisk, until combined. Dollop the sponge mixture over the top of the cherries, spread to a smooth layer, trying not to disturb the cherries underneath too much. Scatter over the flaked almonds, then bake for 45 minutes, until a skewer inserted into the sponge layer comes out clean. Leave to cool for 5 minutes before dusting with icing sugar and serving with cream or, better yet, vanilla custard.

PER SERVING 732 kcals, protein 11g, carbs 65g, fat 48g, sat fat 20g, fibre 1g, sugar 58g, salt 0.8g

Pear parkin pudding

This easy and comforting pud is the perfect way to round off a family lunch.

TAKES 1 HOUR 25 MINUTES
● **SERVES 8**

200g/7oz porridge oats
200g/7oz self-raising flour
2 tsp ground ginger
¼ tsp salt
175g/6oz treacle
140g/5oz butter, plus extra for the dish
   and dotting over
140g/5oz light muscovado sugar, plus
   a bit more
2 balls stem ginger from a jar, chopped,
   plus some of the syrup to drizzle
1 large egg
150ml/¼ pint milk
4 ripe pears, peeled, stalks cut off,
   cored and halved
custard, to serve

1 Heat oven to 160C/140C fan/gas 3. Butter a 30 x 20cm baking dish. Mix the first four ingredients together. Melt the treacle, butter and sugar together in a large pan, then stir in the dry ingredients, half of the chopped ginger, the egg and milk to give a smooth batter.
2 Spoon into the baking dish, then sit the pear halves in the batter. Dot more butter over each pear half and sprinkle with a little more sugar. Bake for 1 hour until risen all over and a skewer inserted into the middle of the pudding comes out clean.
3 To serve, scatter the rest of the ginger over the fruit, then drizzle all over with syrup from the jar. Serve in rectangles with custard.

PER SERVING 538 kcals, protein 9g, carbs 81g, fat 22g, sat fat 13g, fibre 5g, sugar 45g, salt 0.91g

Baked lemon & vanilla rice pudding

The uplifting zing of lemon zest cuts through the richness of this creamy and comforting classic.

TAKES 1 HOUR 40 MINUTES
● **SERVES 6**
600ml/1 pint milk
450ml/16fl oz single cream
zest 1 unwaxed lemon
1 vanilla pod, split
25g/1oz caster sugar
100g/4oz short grain pudding rice
25g/1oz butter, diced

1 Heat oven to 140C/120C fan/gas 1. Put the milk, cream, zest and vanilla pod in a pan. Gently bring to a simmer, then stir in the caster sugar and rice.
2 Transfer the mixture to a shallow ovenproof dish and dot the butter on top. Bake for 30 minutes, then stir well and cook for 1 hour more until the pudding is soft and creamy and a golden skin has formed on top. The depth and type of dish you use will affect the cooking time, so if the pudding seems too loose, return to the oven and check every 10 minutes or so. Once cooked, rest for 10 minutes before serving.

PER SERVING 309 kcals, protein 6g, carbs 27g, fat 20g, sat fat 12g, fibre none, sugar 10g, salt none

Frozen raspberry & white-chocolate cheesecake

This fruity frozen cheesecake is a perfect make-ahead dessert for entertaining.

TAKES 1¼ HOURS, PLUS FREEZING
● **SERVES 15**

oil, for greasing
200ml pot double cream
200g bar white chocolate, broken into chunks, plus extra, melted, to drizzle
300g/11oz raspberries, plus extra to serve
500g/1lb 2oz soft cheese
50g/2oz golden caster sugar
300g/11oz vanilla or white chocolate ice cream (all will taste good, but ice creams without too many chunks are best)

FOR THE BASE

175g/6oz crunchy butter biscuits
140g/5oz ginger nut biscuits
140g/5oz butter, melted

1 Oil a 20 x 30cm baking tin.Line with two layers of cling film, leaving overhang for lifting out. Whizz the biscuits to crumbs in a food processor, then tip in the melted butter and mix again. Press the crumbs firmly into the base of the prepared tin, then chill.

2 Put the cream and chocolate in a small pan. Melt gently, stirring, until no lumps remain. Clean out the food processor and add the raspberries and chocolate mixture. Whizz until smooth, then rub through a sieve to get rid of the seeds.

3 Beat the soft cheese, sugar and the sieved raspberry mixture in a mixing bowl with an electric whisk until smooth.

4 Let the ice cream soften in a big bowl, then gradually fold in the soft-cheese mixture until mixed. Scrape into the prepared tin and level. Cover with cling film, not letting it touch the top of the cheesecake, then freeze overnight.

5 Remove the cling film, lift out the cheesecake. Decorate with raspberries and drizzle with melted white chocolate.

PER SERVING 502 kcals, protein 5g, carbs 30g, fat 40g, sat fat 25g, fibre 1g, sugar 22g, salt 0.7g

Hot-cross-bun bread & lemon pudding

A great way to use up leftover hot cross buns, or use croissants, pain au chocolat or brioche instead.

TAKES 1 HOUR • SERVES 4

knob butter, for the dish
4 stale hot cross buns
200g/7oz lemon curd
2 large eggs
200ml/7fl oz double cream
200ml/7fl oz milk
½ tsp vanilla extract
4 tbsp caster sugar
little lemon zest
cream or vanilla ice cream, to serve
   (optional)

1 Butter a 1-litre baking dish that will quite snugly fit the buns. Cut each bun into three slices, and sandwich back together with a generous spreading of most of the curd. Arrange the buns in the dish.

2 Whisk together the eggs, cream, milk and remaining curd, then sieve into a jug with the vanilla and 3 tablespoons of the sugar. Pour over the buns and stand at room temperature for 30 minutes for the custard to soak in.

3 Heat oven to 160C/140C fan/gas 3. Scatter the remaining sugar and the lemon zest over the pudding. Bake for 30–40 minutes until the top is golden and the custard gently set. Stand for 5 minutes, then serve with cream or vanilla ice cream, if you like.

PER SERVING 676 kcals, protein 10g, carbs 74g, fat 38g, sat fat 20g, fibre 1g, sugar 49g, salt 0.4g

Self-saucing Jaffa pudding

This intense chocolate-orange sponge bake with thick chocolate sauce is about as indulgent as a good pudding gets.

TAKES 1 HOUR 5 MINUTES • SERVES 8

100g/4oz butter, melted, plus a little extra for the dish
250g/9oz self-raising flour
140g/5oz caster sugar
50g/2oz cocoa powder
1 tsp baking powder
zest and juice 1 orange
3 eggs
150ml/¼ pint milk
100g/4oz orange milk chocolate or milk chocolate, broken into chunks
vanilla ice cream or single cream, to serve

FOR THE SAUCE

200g/7oz light muscovado sugar
25g/1oz cocoa powder

1 Butter a 2-litre baking dish and heat oven to 180C/160C fan/gas 4. Put the kettle on. Put the flour, caster sugar, cocoa, baking powder, orange zest and a pinch of salt in a large mixing bowl. Whisk together the orange juice and any pulp left in the juicer, the eggs, melted butter and milk, then pour on to the dry ingredients, and mix together until smooth. Stir in the chocolate chunks and scrape everything into the baking dish.
2 Mix 300ml/½ pint boiling water from the kettle with the sugar and cocoa for the sauce, then pour this all over the pudding batter – don't worry, it will look very strange at this stage! Bake on the middle shelf of the oven for 30 minutes until the surface looks firm, risen and crisp. As you scoop spoonfuls into serving bowls, you should find a glossy, rich chocolate sauce underneath the sponge. Eat immediately with vanilla ice cream or single cream.

PER SERVING 522 kcals, protein 8g, carbs 82g, fat 21g, sat fat 11g, fibre 2g, sugar 54g, salt 0.86g

Patchwork strawberry & gooseberry pie

Tart gooseberries and jammy strawberries make a tasty pair.

TAKES 1 HOUR 40 MINUTES

● **SERVES 10**

FOR THE PASTRY

1 large egg, at room temperature,
  separated
225g/8oz unsalted butter, soft but not
  greasy
1 tsp vanilla extract
50g/2oz caster sugar
½ tsp salt
350g/12oz plain flour, plus extra for
  dusting

FOR THE FILLING

500g/1lb 2oz ripe strawberries, halved,
  or quartered if large
500g/1lb 2oz gooseberries, washed,
  topped and tailed
100g/4oz golden caster sugar, plus
  extra 1 tbsp
1 tsp ground cinnamon
2 tbsp semolina or ground almonds

1 Pulse the egg yolk, butter, vanilla, sugar and salt in a food processor until soft. Add the flour; pulse until the mixture comes together. Squish the dough into two pieces, one slightly larger than the other. Wrap in cling film and chill for 30 minutes.

2 Put the berries and sugar in a wide pan and cook for 5 minutes until syrupy. Drain in a colander over a bowl and cool. Mix the cinnamon and extra sugar, and set aside.

3 Heat oven to 200C/180C fan/gas 6. Roll out the larger piece of pastry to line a 23cm tart tin. Prick several times with a fork, chill until firm, then line with foil and fill with baking beans. Bake on a baking sheet for 15 minutes. Remove the foil and beans, and bake for 10 minutes more. Roll the second pastry disc to roughly the size of the tart and cut into 5cm/2in squares.

4 Scatter the semolina or almonds over the pastry base. Top with the fruit and 2 tablespoons of the syrup. Space pastry squares over the top, brush with egg white, then scatter over most of the cinnamon sugar. Bake for 30 minutes until golden and crisp. Scatter with spiced sugar and serve.

PER SERVING 400 kcals, protein 5g, carbs 51g, fat 20g, sat fat 12g, fibre 4g, sugar 25g, salt 0.3g

Chocolate, pear & marzipan strudel

This strudel couldn't be simpler, and freezes well. Bake from frozen, adding 15 minutes.

TAKES 1 HOUR 10 MINUTES
- **SERVES 6**

85g/3oz butter, melted, plus an
  extra knob
5 pears, peeled and roughly chopped
75g/2½oz light muscovado sugar, plus
  ½ tbsp
2 tsp amaretto (optional)
100g/4oz ginger biscuits, crushed
1 tsp ground cinnamon
100g/4oz dark chocolate, broken into
  chunks
100g/4oz marzipan, chopped into
  small pieces
250g pack filo, at least 6 sheets
icing sugar, to dust
cream, to serve

1 Melt a small knob of the butter in a large frying pan, add the pears and 1 tablespoon of the sugar, then cook for 5 minutes or until just tender. Leave to cool. Put the amaretto, if using, biscuits, cinnamon, chocolate, marzipan, and 2 tablespoons sugar into a bowl; mix well.

2 Line a tray with baking parchment. Lay 1 sheet of filo on the parchment, brush with melted butter and sprinkle with a little sugar. Top with a second layer of filo and keep going until you have used all the pastry. Pile the filling down one of the long sides of the pastry, then roll up to form a sausage. When it's seam-side down, tuck the ends under tightly.

3 Heat oven to 200C/180C fan/gas 6. Place a tray in the oven to heat. Put the strudel, seam-side down, still on its parchment, on the hot tray. Brush all over with melted butter and sprinkle over ½ tablespoon sugar. Bake for 35–40 minutes or until the pastry is golden. Leave to cool for 10 minutes, then dust with icing sugar. Serve with cream.

PER SERVING 521 kcals, protein 5g, carbs 66g, fat 25g, sat fat 14g, fibre 6g, sugar 47g, salt 1.2g

Eton mess trifle

A quintessentially British pudding with sherry-steeped strawberries.

TAKES 40 MINUTES ● **SERVES 6–8**

1 small jam-filled Swiss roll, sliced
450g/1lb strawberries, hulled
seeds from 1 split vanilla pod (save the
    pod for the coulis, below)
2 tbsp icing sugar
500ml/18fl oz double cream
150g pot full-fat natural yogurt
16 ready-made mini meringues (or use
    8 larger meringues broken into
    pieces)
1 tbsp toasted flaked almonds

FOR THE COULIS

140g/5oz strawberries, chopped
2 tbsp golden caster sugar
1 vanilla pod
100ml/3½fl oz sweet sherry

1 First make the coulis. Put all the ingredients in a pan and simmer for a few minutes until the sugar has dissolved and the strawberries have started to soften. Remove the vanilla pod, tip the berries into a blender and whizz until smooth. Sieve into a bowl and leave to cool.

2 Arrange the Swiss-roll slices on the sides and bottom of a large trifle bowl and drizzle over 4 tablespoons of coulis. Save 8 strawberries for the top of the trifle. Cut the rest in half and use some to line the edge of the bowl, cut-side facing out, on top of the Swiss-roll layer. Mix the rest with 2 tablespoons of the coulis.

3 Add the vanilla seeds and icing sugar to the cream and softly whip. Fold in the yogurt and ripple through the coulis. Tip half the cream into the trifle bowl, add the remaining sliced strawberries, then half the meringues. Spoon in the remaining cream. Slice the 8 remaining strawberries into halves or quarters and pop these on top with the remaining meringues and the flaked almonds. Serve immediately.

PER SERVING (8) 515 kcals, protein 5g, carbs 38g, fat 37g, sat fat 22g, fibre 1g, sugar 35g, salt 0.2g

Schooldays' citrus pudding

Use lemon, lime or grapefruit in this squidgy baked dessert – a simple and nostalgic family pud.

TAKES 1 HOUR • SERVES 4

50g/2oz butter, softened, plus extra for greasing
200g/7oz caster sugar
zest 2 lemons or 2 limes or 1 grapefruit
100ml/3½fl oz lemon, lime or grapefruit juice, or a mixture
3 large eggs, separated
50g/2oz plain flour
250ml/9fl oz milk
icing sugar, for dusting (optional)

1 Heat oven to 180C/160C fan/gas 4. Grease a medium-size oval baking dish (we used 22 x 18cm) with butter. Combine the butter, caster sugar and zest in a food processor, and whizz until the mixture is pale. Add the citrus juice, egg yolks, flour and milk, and whizz until well mixed – it may look a little curdled. Scrape into a bowl. Boil the kettle.

2 In a large, clean bowl, whisk the egg whites until firm but not stiff, then gently fold into the zesty mixture. Scrape into the baking dish and put in a roasting tin half-filled with hot water from the kettle. Bake for 35–40 minutes until the top is lightly browned and set, but the pudding is still soft-ish underneath. Serve dusted with icing sugar, if you like.

PER SERVING 432 kcals, protein 8g, carbs 61g, fat 17g, sat fat 9g, fibre 1g, sugar 53g, salt 0.4g

Index

Also available from BBC Books and *Good Food*